A Visitor's Guide to
THE WELSH BORDERS

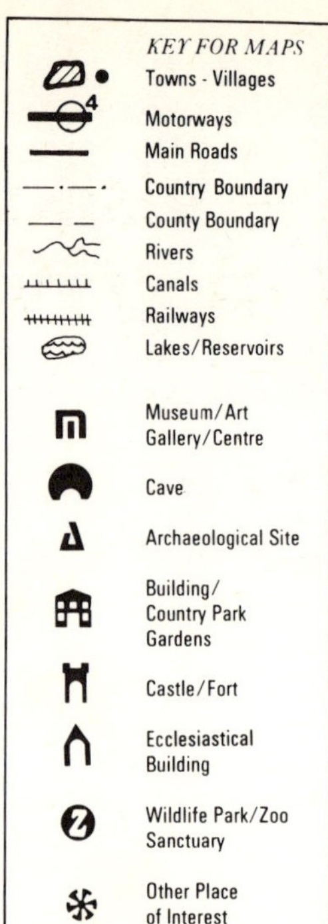

Visitor's Guide Series

This series of guide books gives, in each volume, the details and facts needed to make the most of a holiday in one of the tourist areas of Britain and Europe.

Other titles already published or planned include:
The Lake District (revised edition)
The Peak District
The Chilterns
The Cotswolds
North Wales
The Yorkshire Dales
Cornwall
Devon
Somerset and Dorset
Guernsey, Alderney and Sark
The Scottish Borders
  and Edinburgh
South and West Wales
East Anglia
The North York Moors,
  York and the Yorkshire Coast
Brittany (France)
The South of France
The Black Forest (Germany)
Dordogne (France)

The Visitor's Guide To
THE WELSH BORDERS

Lawrence Garner

British Library Cataloguing
in Publication Data

Garner, Lawrence
    A visitor's guide to the Welsh
    borders.
    1. Borders of Wales — Description
    and travel — Guide-books
    I. Title
    914.24   DA740.B7

All black and white photographs were provided
by the author.

Colour photographs were provided by:
John Robey (Coleham Pumping Engine;
Stokesay Castle) Lawrence Garner (Chirk
Aqueduct; The Wye from Symonds Yat;
Llandegfedd Reservoir; Goodrich Castle). All
others by Ron Scholes.

Front cover:
Andy Williams
Rear cover:
Lawrence Garner

ISBN 0 86190 091 X (hardback)
ISBN 0 86190 090 1 (paperback)

Printed in the UK by
Butler and Tanner Ltd, Frome
for the publishers
Moorland Publishing Co Ltd,
9-11 Station Street, Ashbourne,
Derbyshire, DE6 1DE England.
Telephone: (0335) 44486

Contents

Using this Book

I have followed the format already established in other Guides in this series. Each chapter deals in some detail with a specific area, giving background information and suggesting possible itineraries. For quick reference the main attractions in each area are highlighted by means of insets. In most cases these summarise information given at greater length in the text. Finally there is a comprehensive reference section at the end of the book where the main attractions are classified and essential information (eg times of opening) is included. This information was correct at the time of writing, but obviously changes may occur. Admission charges are not given - unfortunately, these change faster than anything else.

I hope that this arrangement will enable the book to be used both for pre-holiday browsing and for handy reference during the holiday itself.

In each chapter there are suggestions for walks with coded information in the margin. The figure is the approximate length of the walk in miles, and it should be noted that *unless a circular walk is clearly indicated* the distance given is that between the starting point and the objective. The asterisks give some indication of the difficulty of the walk, as follows:

* Gentle stroll
** Suitable for the average active family, suitably clothed and shod
*** Involving some risk, especially in poor visibility. Appropriate clothing and elementary safety precautions
**** For experienced walkers only — compass and full safety precautions needed.

It is assumed that anyone attempting more than a gentle stroll will be equipped with at least a 1in OS map or the metric equivalent.

I should point out that this is the first full holiday guide to the Welsh border. It is an area that does not yet have agreed boundaries, and I have been arbitrary in deciding where it begins and ends. I therefore apologise in advance if the residents of Whitchurch or Llandrindod Wells are offended by the assumption that they live on the border.

However, as a border dweller myself, I think they will want to join me in the hope that all readers of this book will come to sample the pleasures of one of the most fascinating and least-known areas of Britain.

Pant Glas,
Oswestry,

Introduction

The Welsh border offers the holidaymaker more variety in a small space than any other area of Britain. Snowdonia, the Lake District, the Yorkshire Dales or East Anglia, beautiful though they are, each present one kind of landscape, which may or may not be to your taste. The Welsh border has major mountain ranges, pastoral plains, high and undulating moorland, grey towns, picturesque villages of half-timbered houses, a cathedral city, an elegant spa, rich and civilised stately homes, abandoned castles, mines and quarries, broad rivers, remote valleys, some of the most splendid churches and some of the most primitive, the richest agricultural land and the poorest.

This is the language of the holiday brochure, but it is a fact that in the course of a week here you could find yourself in half a dozen totally different environments. The reason has much to do with geography, but perhaps more to do with history.

For most of its length the border is where the plains of Cheshire, Shropshire and Herefordshire abruptly meet the upland barrier that has traditionally ensured the separate identity of Wales. A few rivers — the Usk, the Wye, the Teme, the Severn, and the Dee — have carved out the major routes through the barrier. These simple geographical factors in themselves lead to sharp and sudden contrasts of landscape.

But history has brought its own complications. I am well aware that most readers tend to skip the historical background in this sort of book, but an elementary grasp of history is necessary to understand the strange contrasts of the area.

It was fought over savagely for hundreds of years, and no British countryside has had more blood spilt on it. The people behind the Welsh hills were always a threat to whoever controlled the rich country to the east. The Romans set up border forts of varying duration, and subdued opposition with brisk efficiency, but they showed little enthusiasm for settling in the dangerous Celtic wastes. The Anglo-Saxons resigned themselves to continual border skirmishing until King Offa of Mercia established his famous Dyke towards the end of the eighth century and gave Wales a political border for the first time.

We know almost nothing about the reasons for the Dyke or about its construction. It used to be thought that it was a defensive work, but this idea has been abandoned. Most scholars see it as a simple attempt to mark out a frontier, and they doubt whether it was imposed on the Welsh by superior force. They point out that some Saxon settlements (like Buttington, near Welshpool) were left on the Welsh side, together with some very desirable farming land, and the indications are that the line of the Dyke was negotiated. It can even be seen as a sign of defeat for Offa — the abandonment of any hope of subduing Wales. Whatever the circumstances, it was a spectacular project, stretching from Prestatyn in the north to Chepstow in the south.

The establishment of a border usually

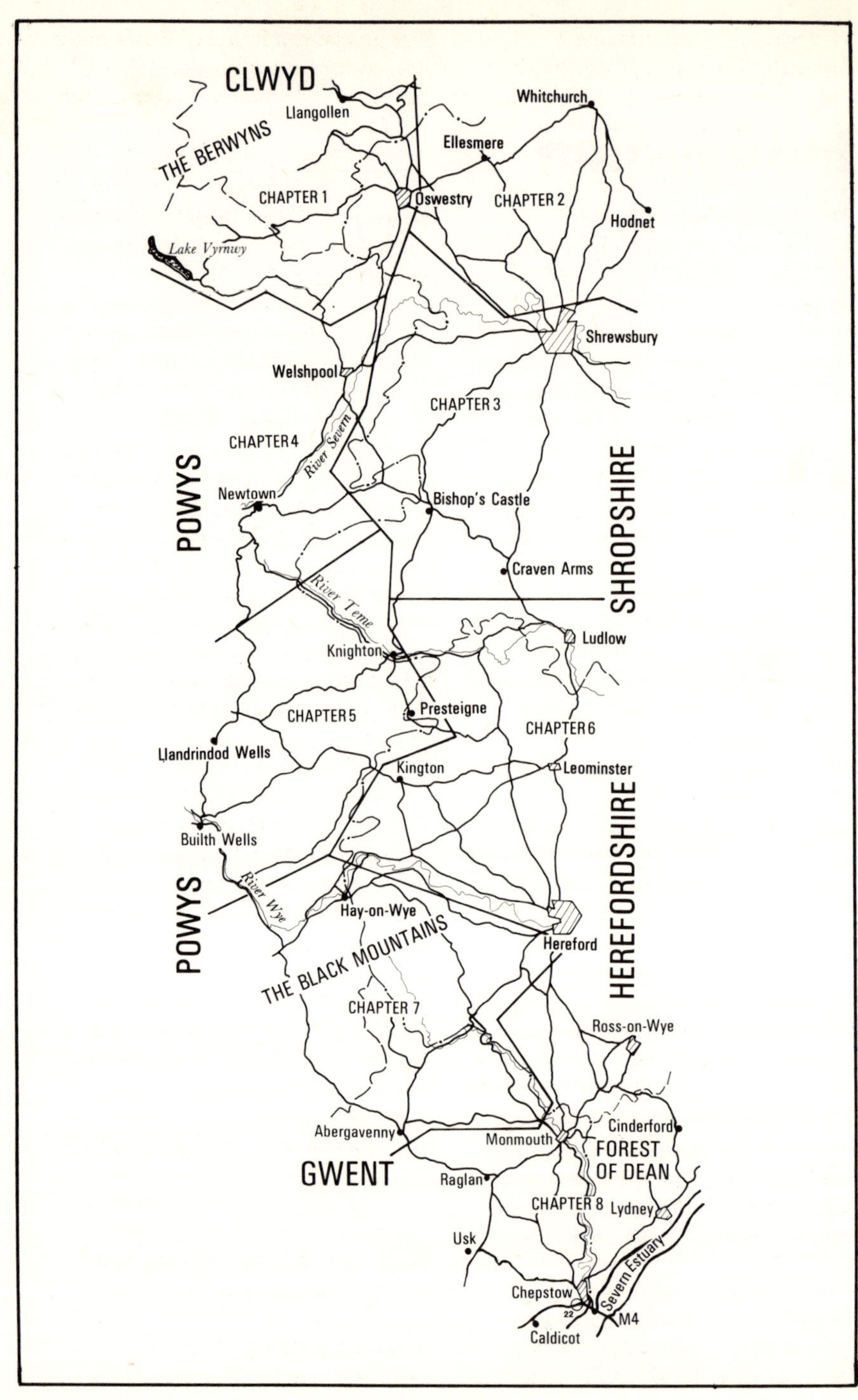

CLWYD
Llangollen
Whitchurch
THE BERWYNS
Ellesmere
CHAPTER 1
Oswestry
CHAPTER 2
Hodnet
Lake Vyrnwy
Shrewsbury
Welshpool
CHAPTER 3
CHAPTER 4
River Severn
POWYS
SHROPSHIRE
Newtown
Bishop's Castle
River Teme
Craven Arms
Ludlow
Knighton
CHAPTER 5
Presteigne
CHAPTER 6
Llandrindod Wells
Kington
Leominster
HEREFORDSHIRE
Builth Wells
River Wye
POWYS
Hay-on-Wye
Hereford
THE BLACK MOUNTAINS
CHAPTER 7
Ross-on-Wye
Cinderford
Abergavenny
Monmouth
FOREST
OF DEAN
GWENT
Raglan
CHAPTER 8
Lydney
Usk
Severn Estuary
Chepstow
22
M4
Caldicot

has the result of encouraging nationalism, and so it proved here. Ever since the departure of the Romans in the fifth century a distinct Celtic culture had been developing, mainly under the influence of the Celtic Church. This was the age of the 'Celtic Saints', the wandering missionaries who gave their names to so many Welsh settlements. Now came a new political awareness, and the scattered Welsh tribes began to unify under a few powerful rulers, including the legendary Princes of Powys, who controlled the central border area.

Unfortunately, while England quietly prospered, Wales became the scene of internal struggles for power, and was in no state to meet the threat of a new enemy, the Normans. After the Conquest the border entered its bloodiest era. William the Conqueror's solution to the Welsh threat was to hand over the border to some of his most formidable followers, giving them virtual independence in return for securing his western frontier.

These great 'Marcher Lords' followed the King's example and subdivided their own territory on the same basis, and the result was a host of petty dictatorships and warring factions. The border became a battleground for some incredibly tangled warfare — Welsh against Welsh, Norman against Norman, Norman against Welsh. To all intents and purposes, it was cut off from English law. The conflict was probably at its worst during the chaotic reign of Stephen, but it was not until Edward I finally gained mastery over Wales in 1282 that a semblance of peace descended.

There was still destruction to come, however. In 1400 a distinguished and civilised country gentleman named Owain Glyndwr (or Owen Glendower)

was proclaimed Prince of Wales, and a desperate revolt against the English began. Glyndwr's aims were idealistic, but he showed no mercy in his campaigns, adopting 'scorched earth' tactics when necessary. His ruthlessness extended to both sides of the border, and the phrase ' laid waste by Owain Glyndwr' occurs with monotonous regularity in the guidebooks. Not until 1485 was stability established with the accession, of a Welshman, Henry VII. The Civil War of the seventeenth century was still to come.

The results of this turbulent history can be seen today. On a superficial level it explains why even insignificant hamlets have the remains of castles, although these would have been little more than wooden palisades built on earth mounds. But it also explains why, for a few miles on each side of the border, there is a distinctive sense of what can only be described as Anglo-Welshness.

It is strongest in the genuine border towns like Oswestry, Montgomery, Knighton, Kington, Presteigne and Hay-on-Wye, which survived against the odds and are still not quite sure which side they are on. The same feeling is likely to extend to anyone living west of Shrewsbury, Leominster, Ludlow or Hereford, because towns like these, far more than the political boundary, marked the beginning of England. They were securely defended and under the protection of powerful families, so that today they show all the signs of a long history of development, especially in their wealth of medieval buildings.

You will not find many medieval buildings in the corresponding Welsh towns. In fact you will find few towns of any size, and most of the buildings will be of the eighteenth century or later. Lacking protection, their growth was stunted. It is a sad fact, too, that so many of the great religious houses of the border country failed to escape the warfare and were in decline even before the Dissolution.

The great variety of this countryside is not, of course, entirely the result of medieval history. Simple economics have played their part. Perhaps the most striking contrast here is between the comfortable, well-developed villages of western Herefordshire, standing on rich soil, and the sparse settlements of Radnor, just across the border, where the terrain allowed only marginal subsistence for sheep. Places like Wigmore, Weobley or Pembridge are not very big but they retain the atmosphere of towns; on the Welsh side Grosmont, New Radnor and Knucklas are definitely villages that never developed, in spite of the considerable status they once had.

Here and there along the border are places that developed in surprisingly distinctive ways. The Ceiriog Valley became a quarrying community of a kind more often found in North Wales, and even today it is an isolated pocket of fierce Welshness. Oswestry became the headquarters of a big railway network. Llandrindod Wells blossomed incongruously as a Victorian spa, while Church Stretton acquired its own unique atmosphere as an Edwardian health resort. Newtown once rivalled Leeds and Bradford as a woollen town, and Craven Arms grew up as a convenient place to load sheep on to railway trucks.

It is this endless variety and power to surprise that has always attracted the discerning visitor to the border, and the signs are that the area is becoming increasingly popular. It will never rival the Welsh coasts or Snowdonia as a tourist region, because it does not lay out its attractions — it is an intricate and rather secret landscape that has to be explored. Fortunately more and more people are becoming explorers. They are not content with lying on the beach or gazing mutely at 'beautiful scenery'. They have interests to pursue — architecture, wildlife, agriculture, industrial archeology, or simply the business of discovering the unexpected.

Within the limited scope of this book I have tried to point out some of the rewards of exploration, but I am well aware that I have only scratched the surface. It is encouraging to see that local organisations are now producing town and village 'trails', walking guides and other 'private-enterprise' literature to fill the enormous gaps in the official tourist publications, in which the border has always been regarded as a no-man's-land.

On reflection, perhaps that is how it should remain. As the popular holiday areas choke on their own commercialism, the Welsh border will continue to extend an unobtrusive welcome to the discriminating visitor who wants to create his own holiday and reject the ready-made.

1 Llangollen, Oswestry and the Berwyn Valleys

For the thousands of visitors who travel each year on the A5, Chirk is the gateway to Wales, and it serves as a good starting point for an exploration of the northern valleys of the Berwyn mountain area.

Chirk itself is a curious place — an overgrown village, whose efforts to get bigger have resulted in unlovely housing estates and large factories. It is a moot point among the inhabitants as to which produces the worst smell, the cocoa plant or the chipboard works.

The original village, clustered around the fifteenth-century church, retains some charm, but its main attraction lies at an aristocratic distance. Chirk Castle is rare among border fortresses in being virtually intact and inhabited. Owned now by the National Trust, it is still the home of the Myddleton family, who have lived there since 1595. You reach it by way of the road behind Chirk War Memorial — designed by Eric Gill — and it makes its presence known with a magnificent set of eighteenth-century wrought iron gates. They were the masterpiece of the famous Davies brothers of Wrexham.

After a $1\frac{1}{2}$m drive through the park you enter the castle in the most authentic way possible. A portcullis gate leads into an enclosed quadrangle, and even today the sense of security inside is strong. The tour begins with an interesting armoury and a display of historical documents,

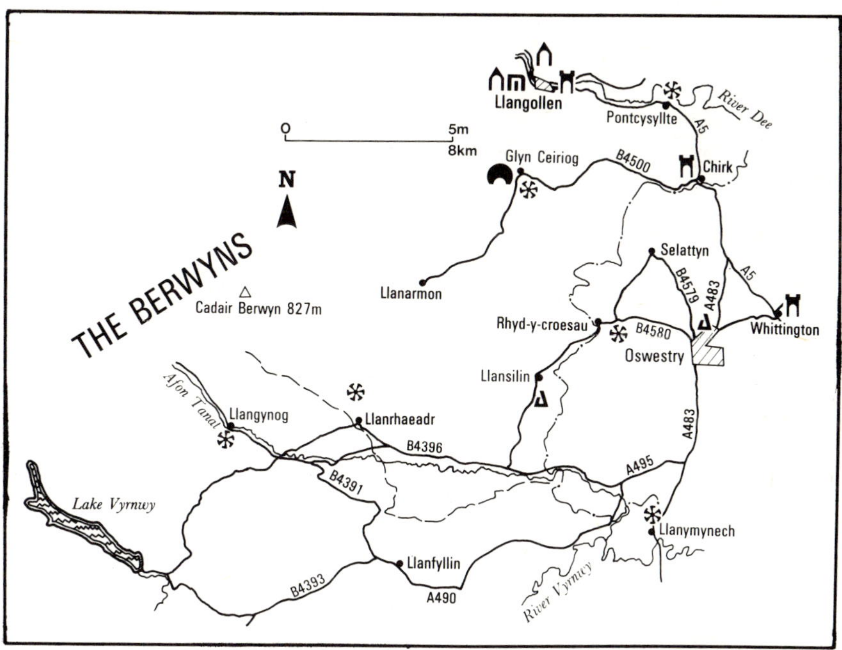

Canal and railway crossings at Chirk

and proceeds through rooms of a luxury that belies the stark exterior. For many people the highlight of the visit is the reconstructed servants' hall, its spartan atmosphere made more severe by the schedule of fines for such offences as swearing and malicious gossip. The superb gardens should not be missed.

Back at the gates there is a choice of routes to Llangollen. The lane to the left as you emerge will take you through the Ceiriog Forest and over a deserted mountain road. As you climb through the trees and emerge on to a ridge at the top, a sensational panorama unfolds, stretching from the South Shropshire hills on the extreme right to distant North Wales on the left. Directly ahead is the scarred industrial landscape of the former mining and iron-making area south of Wrexham. Today the scene is dominated by the giant Monsanto chemical works at Cefn Mawr. After a few more miles of steep hills and sharp bends you drop almost literally into Llangollen.

If you have the slightest suspicion that the car may break down you should return from the castle gates to the A5 and continue on it to Llangollen. It is a fast run along one side of the Dee valley and has the merit of opening up the landscape slowly. The only major village on the way is Froncysyllte, with large lime-kilns on the right of the road and cottages scattered at random on the steep hillside to the left.

The first view of Llangollen can be disappointing. To be honest, it is a rather ordinary, grey town and an unlikely venue for the annual International Eisteddfod. In the summer it teems with tourists, attracted by some natural features and by some astutely man-made ones. Everyone gravitates sooner or later to the Dee Bridge — rightly so, because after a rainy spell the river runs spectacularly fast over foaming rapids and has become a challenge to canoeists. The bridge was built originally in the fourteenth century but has been haphazardly improved many times since, perhaps accounting for its highly irregular appearance.

Below the bridge on the north side is the former railway station, looking dangerously close to the torrent; it must have been a wonderful place to arrive at for a holiday. The station and a short length of track have been taken over by an energetic preservation society, and it is possible to take a nostalgic stroll on a platform which is unmistakeably Great Western. Restoring railways is a passion in Wales second only to singing.

On the hillside above the station another form of transport has been revived. The Llangollen arm of the Shropshire Union Canal runs along its contour line here, and a canal exhibition centre has been set up. There is an excellent small museum and display, with a shop selling not only the inevitable souvenirs but a wide range of canal literature. If you want to sample canal transport in its original form, you can ride on a horse-drawn narrow boat.

As you return across the bridge one of the first buildings on the right is a restored cornmill, complete with waterwheel. It is used now for textile weaving, and demonstrations of old handlooms can be arranged. A little further up, past the Town Hall, it is worth turning right into Market Street to visit the new European Research Centre for Folk Studies, housed in a converted school. The forbidding name

The station yard Llangollen

conceals a cheerful place, staging exhibitions of traditonal crafts and all aspects of popular culture.

You are bound sooner or later to hear about the Ladies of Llangollen. They were Lady Eleanor Butler and Miss Sarah Ponsonby, who came from Ireland in 1779, settled in the town and lived there until they died. They were inseparable friends of eccentric habits, including the wearing of masculine dress, and a visit to their house became something of a status symbol in the early nineteenth century. Among their distinguished visitors were the Duke of Wellington, Sir Walter Scott and William Wordsworth. It was the custom to bring the Ladies a piece of wood-carving as a present; the story is that Wordsworth's gift of a sonnet was rather sniffed at.

Their house, Plas Newydd, is high above the town, but before climbing to it you can go up Church Street to St Collen's Church to see their memorial outside the door. The church itself is of twelfth-century foundation with much nineteenth-century enlargement and restoration. The outstanding feature is its carved roof, reputed to have come from nearby Valle Crucis Abbey. Lady Eleanor died in 1829, and Miss Sarah two years later, and their memorial commemorates them with slightly fulsome piety. The stone also includes a tribute to one of their faithful servants.

By continuing up Church Street you emerge directly opposite Butler Hill, which leads to Plas Newydd. The grounds are beautifully kept, and feature a stone circle placed there for the Gorsedd ritual of the 1908 National Eisteddfod. The Ladies loved all forms of woodcarving and employed a local craftsman to embellish the exterior of the house with a vaguely Tudor effect. The result is intricate and undoubtedly

individual.

Beyond Plas Newydd there is a superb view of Dinas Bran Castle, flanked by the limestone crags known as the Eglwseg Rocks. In spite of its romantic position the castle never had much historical significance. It was built in about 1250 on the site of a Bronze Age fort by the Prince of Powys, and when Edward I abolished the princedom in 1282 the castle ceased to be of practical use and gradually fell into ruins. There is a signposted footpath to it, reached by crossing the canal bridge a little way east of the canal exhibition centre. A round walk is possible by going east along the towpath to the bridge where the canal goes under the A539. Turn left here on to a track which works its way round the back of Dinas Bran and then to the top, after which there is a direct path back to the town.

4½
**

It is also simple to walk to Valle Crucis Abbey. One well-known guide book describes this as 'a majestic ruin in a lovely sequestered valley', but its author obviously failed to note the caravan site next door. Nevertheless the ruins *are* majestic and well worth a visit. The abbey was founded in 1201 for Cistercian monks, but failed to survive the Reformation; the ruins that remain hint at a very extensive establishment. For most of the way the walk from the town is by means of the towpath, this time going in a westerly direction. A little way beyond the ruins, close to the main road, are the remains of a wayside cross which once dominated the valley. Now known as Eliseg's Pillar, it was erected in the ninth century in memory of an early Prince of Powys. After being broken up by the Puritans, the remains were re-erected in 1779, and there is a story that a grave and skeleton were found on the spot.

2½
*

On the way back it is a good idea to

walk further along the towpath to the Horseshoe Falls, engineered by Thomas Telford to feed water from the Dee into the canal. Telford figures largely in the history of this area; apart from his ambitious Holyhead Road, now the A5, he carried out some brilliant canal works to extend the Ellesmere Canal to Llangollen, and these can be inspected by leaving Llangollen on the A539 and turning right after about two miles at the Bryn Howel Hotel. This minor road immediately crosses the canal, and a cautious drive will bring you to the River bridge at Trevor, from which the Pontcysyllte Aqueduct can be seen above the trees, carrying boats in mid-air across the Dee. If you ignore the bridge and continue up the steep hill into Trevor it is possible to park the car and walk into the canal basin at the point where the Llangollen arm joins the Shropshire Union.

The towpath takes you straight on to the aqueduct. It is a cast-iron trough 1,000 feet long and 120 feet high, supported on nineteen slender sandstone arches, and built between 1794 and 1805 as Telford's characteristically bold solution to the problem of getting the canal across the deep river valley. The walk is not recommended for anyone nervous of heights, but if you manage it you can return to Trevor by crossing an interesting canal bridge a few hundred yards along from the other side and

PLACES OF INTEREST IN AND AROUND LLANGOLLEN

Canal Museum and Exhibition Centre
Displays showing canal history and technology. Bookstall and souvenir shop. Trips in horse-drawn narrow boat.

Plas Newydd, $\frac{1}{2}$m south of town centre
House of the 'Ladies of Llangollen'.

Castell Dinas Bran
Ruins on steep hill to north of town. Accessible by waymarked path near Canal Centre.

Valle Crucis Abbey, $1\frac{1}{2}$m east of town
Accessible by A542 or by walking along towpath.
Extensive ruins of Cistercian Abbey.

Llangollen Station, below river bridge
Restored steam railway. Train trips sometimes available.

Llangollen Motor Museum, Sun Service Garage, Regent Street
Working garage, engaged in restoring cars.

European Research Centre for Folk Studies, Market Street
Exhibitions on folk studies and craft work. Also workshop and courses.

Llangollen Weavers, south side of bridge
Old cornmill, with waterwheel, now converted to weaving mill. Demonstrations of weaving on old handlooms. Products for sale.

Llangollen Pottery, Regent Street
Domestic stoneware production and sales. Visitors welcome.

Pontcysyllte, Trevor, 5m east of town
Telford's canal aqueduct. Towpath accessible from Trevor canal basin. 120ft high, 1000ft long.

*Thomas Telford's canal aqueduct over the
Dee at Poncysyllte*

joining the road which dips sharply
down to the river, offering a good view
of the aqueduct from ground level.

Chirk is a short distance by car, but
the canal enthusiast will certainly want
to do the journey on foot and examine
the other canal works along this stretch.
After crossing the aqueduct, simply
carry on along the towpath, passing
some lime-kilns on the other bank.
(Much of the locally-produced limestone
was used for dressing fields and needed
to be burnt. Since the natural lime
damaged canal boats it was usual to
burn it before loading — hence the kilns
found at many points on canal banks.)

The path is badly-maintained in
places but usable with care. After a short
tunnel, the canal skirts the grounds of
Chirk Castle, passes the backs of the
new Chirk factories and reaches the
famous Chirk tunnel. A torch is essential
here, because the path and handrail are
unreliable and the daylight does not
penetrate to the middle. On emerging
you cross another aqueduct, built earlier
than the famous one to take the canal
across the Ceiriog river. A railway
viaduct, not by Telford, is only a few
yards away. By leaving the towpath at
the Chirk Bank bridge you can return to
Chirk by the main road, which gives an
excellent view of the parallel rail and
canal structures.

In view of their proximity there is a
remarkable difference between the
Llangollen and Ceiriog valleys. The
former has something of the atmosphere
of a Victorian resort, a meeting-place for
respectable tourists of antiquarian
interests. The latter is steeped in the
blood, sweat and poverty of the mining
and quarrying industries.

You can get to the Ceiriog valley

3½
**

(pronounced 'kerryog') by an
adventurous road over the mountains
from Llangollen, but in many ways it is
better to take the unexciting-looking
road opposite the church at Chirk. You
then have the sense of passing from an
open, pastoral landscape into a closed
community. The road follows the river
uneventfully for some time, but at
Pontfadog, the first village in the valley,
the Berwyns begin to loom in the
distance, and from then on you travel
into hills reminiscent of Snowdonia.

The best way of exploring the valley is
to drive directly to Llanarmon at the far
end and then return slowly. Llanarmon
is a tiny outpost; although two mountain
roads lead out of it, it is very much the
'end of the line'. Dominating it are the
West Arms and the Hand Hotel, two
inns with humble backgrounds still
detectable under a good deal of
expensive and picturesque modernisation.

In 1846 Llanarmon's most famous son
was fourteen years old. He was John
Hughes, who started his working life
locally as a farmhand and rose to
become a station-master and railway
manager. More to the point, he became
one of Wales's most famous bards,
taking the name 'Ceiriog' and gaining a
reputation as 'The Robert Burns of
Wales'. Outside Wales he is probably
best known as the author of the original
words of 'Men of Harlech' and 'God
Bless the Prince of Wales'. His
birthplace, Pen-y-Bryn, can still be seen
to the east of the village.

From its centre the roads to Llansilin
and Llanrhaeadr are good scenic drives.
The third road, marked 'no through
road', is the starting point for a whole
network of walks traversing the Berwyn
mountains. They are marked on the
Ordnance Survey map, but it must be
stressed that the Berwyns are deserted
and potentially dangerous — certainly

not to be under-estimated. Anything
more than a short stroll should be
undertaken only by those who are fit
and suitably clothed.

A not-too-demanding walk is possible
from the hamlet of Tregeiriog, about a
mile from Llanarmon along the valley
road. By taking the lane to the north you
can climb to about 1,500 feet. Soon after
the track becomes a footpath, you reach
a lane, at which you should turn left and
follow it down towards a ford. Just
before the ford, there is a path on the left
which brings you back down beside a
stream. You rejoin the main road soon
after passing the Hafod Adams farm.

Back on the main road out of
Tregeiriog the view on the right is
screened by trees which in summer
conceal the sight of the fearsome Hendre
granite quarry, opened in 1875 to
provide blocks for road and tramway
construction. It lasted until 1950, by
which time some three million tons of
stone had been extracted. You can get a
closer view of the workings and of some
smaller sites by walking along the
trackbed of the old tramway which
served them. About half a mile before
the next village, Pandy, there is a lane to
the right, crossing the river at the Pont-
y-Meibion bridge. (The farmhouse on
the left of the road opposite the bridge
was the birthplace of another, older
bard, Huw Morris.) The trackbed can be
followed from here to Hendre. and there
are smaller workings on both sides of the
river.

A mile beyond Pandy lies Glyn
Ceiriog, the valley's main settlement.
There is very little indication today of
what it must have looked like in its
heyday as a quarry village. Some houses
and walls still show their quarry-waste
construction, but many others have been
smartened up with cement rendering.
The High Street, leading up from the

junction of five roads, remains a narrow, intimate lane, and peters out at the church to become a minor road to Llangollen.

The high, forested hills overshadowing the village are deceptive; the roots of the trees are growing through slate waste, and a close look will reveal the scree marking the old workings. Two sites on these hills — the Cambrian and Wynne quarries — were the source of Glyn Ceiriog's former importance and prosperity. Slate was extracted here for a thousand years, but the period of heavy exploitation was from the 1850s to the end of the First World War. It finally ceased in 1946 when some of the workings flooded.

There is an excellent opportunity to find out more about the history and working of these quarries by visiting the museum and exhibition housed on the old Wynne quarry site. Chwarel Wynne, as it is called, can be reached by car (parking at the Plas Owen Hotel) or on foot by a lane to the left off the High Street. Anyone seriously interested in industrial archaeology may find Chwarel Wynne more rewarding than the more famous slate museums of North Wales because it caters mainly for educational visits. Casual visitors are welcome, however, and there are periodic tours underground to reconstructed workings.

The striking thing about Glyn Ceiriog is its intense Welshness, unusual so close to the border. The reason, of course, is its long existence as a tightly-knit working community, cut off in many ways from the wider world a few miles beyond. There was poverty and great danger, but there was also a devotion to culture; the quarry villages, here and elsewhere, were traditionally centres of musical and literary study. Nowhere is this more vividly shown than in the Memorial Institute, erected to the memory of the bard John Hughes.

The Institute is a short way up the High Street on the left, and is normally open to visitors. Basically it is a village hall, but it is like no other village hall, with its busts of famous local men, its memorial plaques and its display of books, pamphlets and other evidence of the pursuit of self-education. It is pleasant to see a whole stained-glass window dedicated to the memory of a local doctor. There is a memorial to yet another bard, Robert Ellis, and also to Lancelot Hogben, author of 'Science for the Citizen', who was a resident of the valley. There are few more fascinating buildings in Wales than this unobtrusive hall.

Mention has been made of a tramway serving the quarries, and at the Glyn Valley Hotel a small exhibition has been set up to commemorate this curious line. A line with horse-drawn wagons was established in the 1870s and converted to steam in 1888, when a nine-mile length of track carried mineral traffic to canal and main-line railway points near Chirk. Passengers were carried from 1891, and the line survived until 1935.

The Glyn Valley Tramway was always a picturesque affair, not only because of its scenery but because its locomotives were a combination of railway engine and tram. But it was a vital link for the industry and people of the valley, carrying 30,000 tons of minerals a year at its peak.

After the seclusion of the Ceiriog Valley, it comes as something of a shock to return to Chirk and be confronted with the congested A5 again. However, there is no need to go further than Oswestry to explore two more of these Berwyn valleys, which remain comparatively little-known. So far we have remained firmly in Wales, but in moving the short distance south we reach more typical border country where the national boundary ceases to mean very much and a fellow-feeling exists among people on both sides. This spirit is exemplified in Oswestry, an Anglo-Welsh town where the Wednesday markets bring a bi-lingual crowd spilling on to the streets.

Oswestry makes no claims to beauty, but quietly carries out its function of providing commercial, social and educational facilities to a wide area of the surrounding countryside. It derives its name from 'Oswald's Tree' — a reference to the fate of King Oswald of Northumbria, who was defeated here by Penda of Mercia in 642 and whose body was nailed to a tree. Because of its position right on the border, Oswestry was the scene of much strife and destruction, not to mention a series of fires, with the result that there are few early buildings in the town.

It does, however, possess one of the biggest Iron Age hill forts in the country. Hen Dinas, or Old Oswestry, lies on the northern outskirts of the town, and is approached rather incongruously through a council estate. 100ft high and 15 acres in extent, it has a complex series of defence works which can be walked over freely. It is worth a visit for the views over the town and surrounding countryside; in fact you can see from here three features that have at various times brought fame to Oswestry.

To the north, marked by a tall chimney, is the world-famous orthopaedic hospital, the founding of

which is referred to in the next chapter.
Further south, and almost adjoining it,
is Park Hall, once an estate with an
impressive half-timbered house and
more recently a sprawling army camp.
There are hundreds of middle-aged ex-
national servicemen who have mixed
memories of the Royal Artillery basic
training depot here. The military moved
out some years ago, and Park Hall is
now being restored to various kinds of
civilian use. Thirdly there is the former
station area, with its red-brick
engineering workshops.   It is difficult
to believe now that Oswestry was once
one of the major railway centres of
Britain. The first line arrived here in
1848, and by 1866 the town had become
the headquarters of the Cambrian
Railways, with extensive locomotive and
carriage works. Cambrian became one

of the biggest rail networks outside the
'Big Four'; at its peak the system
extended almost to Brecon in the south
and across to Aberystwyth in the west.
There was a maze of lines around
Oswestry itself to service the important
mineral industry in the area. The station
closed in the mid-sixties but the dignified
administrative building is still there, and
next to it is the yard of the ambitious
Cambrian Railways Society, which is
restoring locomotives and rolling stock
in the hope of running trains again on
the remaining stretch of line.

In the town itself some of the best
buildings are grouped around the parish
church, which was largely rebuilt in the
seventeenth century after extensive fire
damage during the Civil War. It is large,
and unusually square in shape, and the
interior features an imposing Yale

family monument and some interesting memorial brasses. Outside there are some distinguished iron gates and a seventeenth-century lychgate that originally led to the town's grammar school. The half-timbered building in the churchyard (now being converted into a museum) is reputed to be part of the school, established in the fifteenth century.

Directly opposite the church the Wynnstay Hotel stands as a handsome example of a late-Georgian coaching inn. Church Street leads back to the Cross, the centre of the town, and from here two roads can be taken. Bailey Street, with the timber-framed Llwyd Mansion at the bottom, climbs to the site of the open-air market and also to the castle mound. Willow Street leads out of the town and is the route to be taken for a tour of the Tanat Valley and the countryside south-west of Oswestry.

At the top of Willow Street the road (B4579, signposted Selattyn) branches to the right and leaves the town quickly, climbing gently to give a view of Old Oswestry on the right. Shortly before entering Selattyn there is a splendid panorama of the Shropshire Plain. Selattyn itself is a good example of a border hill village, scattered over the foothills of the Berwyns and partly concealed in a deep valley to the north. You look down on the church here with its subtly-coloured stone and distinctive tiled roof; inside there is some fine timbering and an elaborately carved barrel ceiling. The Cross Keys nearby retains an authentic village inn atmosphere.

4½
**

Selattyn is the centre of some good walking country, with interesting contrasts in landscape. After taking the narrow lane almost opposite the school and keeping left after a hundred yards at the fork, you descend rapidly into the valley of the Morlas Brook. If you turn right at the first junction and left at the next crossroads, you find yourself on a peaceful lane with a commanding view across the valley. Turn left at the next fork on to a road which leads gently downhill, with woods to the right and a steep drop to the left, until it reaches the tiny Craignant Chapel, still in use. It now climbs steeply to the main road where the Offa's Dyke path is indicated opposite. The path here is a rutted track that climbs steadily until you emerge on the top of the ridge and find sweeping views to the south. After about a mile of open heathland, you turn left on to a metalled lane which leads back to the village.

The main road through Selattyn goes on to become a scenic route into the Ceiriog Valley, but if you leave by the minor road that climbs away almost opposite the pub, you arrive, after 1½m, at Carreg-y-Byg Farm, a noted landmark for Dyke Path walkers. Just before the farm there is a view to the right of a well-preserved section of Dyke across an exposed field. Turn left at Carreg-y-Byg and climb the steep hill on to Oswestry's Old Racecourse. It was last used as such in 1848, and now provides a public open space famous for the spectacular views over mid-Wales. The car park is reached a few hundred yards after crossing the Oswestry-Llansilin road, and from there the Offa's Dyke path passes through one of its most attractive sections, due south to the bottom of Candy Woods. It makes an attractive stroll in the summer, partly along an exposed ridge and partly through mature trees, with the Dyke very close above the path.

2½
*

From the Racecourse the Llansilin road (B4580) descends via hairpin bends to the village of Rhydycroesau, standing right on the border. The most noticeable

house here is the vast old Rectory, now a
hotel, seen across the valley on the left
soon after passing the church (a rather
smaller building!).

The road between here and Llansilin
lies along one side of the ravine-like
valley of the Cynllaith, and off to the
right there are a good many old lanes
and tracks passing over the hills to the
Ceiriog valley. A glance at the map will
show many opportunities for fitter
walkers.

Llansilin is a remarkably well-
developed village for such an isolated
spot. The narrow roads of the older part
give it an intimate atmosphere, and the
small, low houses reveal some very
individual features. The church of St
Silin is full of interest. It was visited by
George Borrow, who came to see (and
kiss) the tomb of his idol, the bard Huw
Morris, who is buried in the churchyard.
In the south wall of the chancel is a
thirteenth-century lancet window with
an unusual arch carved from a single
piece of stone, and the fine timber roof-
work is fifteenth century. Other interior
features include a seventeenth-century
poor-box and font, and a superb early-
Victorian brass chandelier. On the
outside, the south door is pockmarked
with holes reputed to be the result of
bullets fired when the church was
fortified during the Civil War, and
another unique feature is the line, used
by villages, for the game of 'fives', which
can be seen on the north wall.

The Wynnstay Inn is one of several in
this area with the same name — a
reminder of the influence of the
powerful Williams-Wynn family, whose
main house was Wynnstay, near
Ruabon, but who also owned a mansion
south of Llansilin. Opposite the Inn is a
malthouse of 1822 with a hoist and steps
leading off the road.

A well-mapped walk in the hills to the

west of Llansilin can be taken by turning
up the Llanarmon road opposite the
Post Office and taking the first lane to
the left, which passes Moeliwrch and
Pentre. Turn right when it joins a
metalled road and walk the mile and a
half past Lake Moelfre to the next
crossroads. A right turn here past Fron
takes you round the back of Gyrn
Moelfre (1700 feet) and back to
Moeliwrch.

Shortly after leaving Llansilin, the
B4580 branches right, at a crossroads,
but if you go straight on, you arrive after
2m at a fascinating historical site. As
you descend into a valley with a tiny
crossroads at the bottom you see on
your left a flat-topped mound against a
background of thick conifers. It is all
that remains of Llys Sycharth, the
principal residence of Owain Glyndwr.
There is a famous poem of 1390 by the
poet Iolo describing the great timber hall
with an encircling moat, the parks, the
fishponds, cultivated fields and the rich

5½
**

22

life-style enjoyed there. The castle, burned down in 1402, has been excavated, and the resulting evidence certainly points to a large timber building, however undramatic the site may look today.

A mile further on, you drop down to the junction with the B4396 and turn right at the handsome Green Inn, to arrive at the scattered village of Llangedwyn. The elegant church, on the left, with its unusual dormer windows, has a car park in front, providing a chance to stop and look at several features of interest. The church was completely restored in 1869 and some good stained glass in pre-Raphaelite style was incorporated, but an effigy of a priest forms a link with the fourteenth century. Immediately opposite the church are the impressive gates and walls of Llangedwyn Hall, originally Elizabethan, but altered in the eighteenth century. It was the home of the Williams-Wynn family mentioned earlier. Robert Southey wrote his poem 'Madoc' here, and Bishop Heber was inspired by the playing of an old Welsh harpist to write his famous hymn 'God who madest earth and Heaven, darkness and light'.

6
******
The view to the north west is dominated by the massive Bryn Dinas with a hill fort on its summit. The rather gentler hills to the south provide a chance of an invigorating walk, starting at a lane to the left 2m from Llangedwyn Church. It leads down to a bridge over the Tanat Valley Railway, mentioned later. A bridle path leads away to the left, skirting a wood, and joins a track passing Fron Goch and meeting a metalled road at GR 163233. Turn left and follow the road towards Bwlchyddar. Just before the road junction in the village take a turning to the right up to Mynydd-y-Glyn (1276 feet). Continue over to a track leading down via Croniarth Farm to Glantanat Isaf, where there is a castle mound. From here it is a short distance back to the river and your starting point.

Back on the road, take the right fork after a mile and enter the grey stone village of Llanrhaeadr-yn-Mochnant, passing the tiny school where the decorum was preserved by separate entrances clearly marked 'Boys' and 'Girls'. There is some parking space in the tiny square (which is actually triangular) but more up the Llansilin road leading away to the right.

Like Llansilin this is an intimate place, almost a miniature village, but it usually has the lively air of a rural centre even when the tourists have gone. There are some useful shops, including one of those old-fashioned ironmongers selling almost anything, and even a boutique. A walk up the main street reveals a surprisingly wide range of architectural styles and building materials, and there is a good half-timbered house (rare around here) off Church Street.

St Dogfan's Church is less famous than one of its incumbents. Dr William Morgan became vicar here in 1572 and remained for 23 years, during which he completed his great self-imposed task of translating the Bible into Welsh. It was finished in 1588, the year of the Spanish Armada, but in Welsh history it was a far more significant event than a mere naval victory. There is little doubt that Morgan's translation was the biggest single contribution to the survival of the Welsh language — more often than not it was the only book a household possessed. In the mid-nineteenth century George Borrow remarked on its central position in Welsh culture. Dr Morgan, who was not always at ease with his parishioners, went on to become Bishop of St Asaph.

The church dates from the twelfth century and has been considerably enlarged and restored, particularly in the fifteenth and nineteenth centuries. One of the more interesting later discoveries was a grave slab, possibly of the tenth century, built into the wall of the south aisle.

Few visitors linger to enjoy the atmosphere of this village, which somehow manages to feel like a small town; most of them give it a fleeting glance before turning off the main street to make the 4m trip to the celebrated waterfall, Pistyll Rhaeadr. The indefatigable Borrow did so too, after staying at the Wynnstay Arms. Over a hundred years ago it was a compulsory tourist attraction. In the summer the approach to it can be nerve-wracking because the road was hardly designed for a stream of two-way traffic; it can be frustrating, too, to arrive there and find that a prolonged dry spell has reduced the flow to something less than sensational. At least you do not yet have to pass through a turnstile. A small bridge has been built at the bottom to provide a view of the 240-foot drop, which is obstructed by a natural arch half-way down. It is possible to climb to the top by way of a path from the car park, but the result is distinctly disappointing, since all you see is a narrow stream falling rather casually over the edge with no hint of the thunderous effect at the bottom.

4½
***
A more rewarding walk starts at the waterfall bridge. Cross to the western side of the stream, pass through a small wood and follow the path along some old mining levels until it meets a track coming up from below. The route then lies in a south-westerly direction and passes between the mountains Y Cogydd and Glanhafron. The descent brings you on to a minor road east of Llangynog.

This walk provides a chance to look at various relics of the quarrying and mining industries. (On all walks among these hills a map and compass is essential.)

10
****
Of similar interest to industrial archaeologists is a walk which is reached by going back on the Llanrhaeadr road and turning left for Maengwynedd about a mile before the village. This road takes you even further into the heart of the mountains and comes to an end at Blaen-y-cwm (GR 097322). The road continues as a track for a mile then divides at the former Maengwynedd slate mines. The fork to the right is part of a Bronze Age track — Fford Gam Elin — and if followed through will bring you down into the Dee valley near Llandrillo.

9½
****
An alternative is to take the left fork and follow the path west and then north on to the Berwyn crags. The crags run south and taken in Cader Berwyn (over 2700 feet). A descent can be made to Llyn Lluncaws on the eastern side, and by following a stream out of the lake you link up with a path which brings you to Pistyll Rhaeadr. This is remote and severe country, and definitely for experienced walkers only.

If you do not feel inclined to walk too far, an interesting hour or two can be spent exploring the old mine workings. The track from Blaen-y-cwm passes the remains of miners' houses at the point where Fford Gam Elin branches off. If you continue on the left fork, there are remains of the trimming sheds and a viaduct over a waterway which had a dam just above it. Various workings can be seen, but it is not advisable to be too ambitious in exploring them. Even if industrial relics do not interest you, this is superb mountain country and well worth the drive to reach it.

On returning to Llanrhaeadr turn

right at the main street and take the steep road out of the village towards Penybontfawr. You join the B4391 at the Railway Inn and make for Llangynog round the base of the domed Cyrniau hill. Very soon the scarred and scree-covered Craig Rhiwarth appears on the other side of the valley and you enter Llangynog across a narrow bridge.

Llangynog is one of those villages that came into existence solely to support the quarrying and mining industries. Lead, slate, granite and phosphate were all produced here at various times from the Bronze Age onwards, and the Cyrniau mines on the south side of the village contained the largest vein of lead ever discovered in Britain. More immediately visible there today is the later granite quarry established on the same site. On the other side of the village the huge, dark mass of Craig Rhiwarth is covered with tipped waste through which very little vegetation has managed to grow. There were lead mines here too, although the slate is more evident.

The caravan park on the north bank of the river behind the garage is the site of the former terminus of the Tanat Valley Light Railway — if you look beyond the caravans you can see the embankment leading away up the valley. Among the caravans one platform has been incorporated into the landscaping.

The building of the TVLR caused much acrimonious debate, local rivalry and over-ambition. In 1860 a plan was drawn up to make the Tanat Valley a main line to the west coast, a scheme that was quickly dropped when the estimate for tunnelling under the Berwyns was received. The Light Railways Act of 1896 made possible cheaper standards of construction (although the line was always standard gauge) and work was begun in 1901 on a 15m length to link with the Cambrian Railways line at Llanymynech and go through to Oswestry. It was thought that the lead mines would provide most of the revenue, but by the time the line was ready — construction took three years

Craig Rhiwarth,
Llangynog

because of flooding problems — the mines were beginning to close. Agricultural and passenger traffic kept it going until after the First World War, when there was an expansion of mineral traffic, but by 1921 it was almost bankrupt. It was taken on by the GWR and later by British Rail, but finally closed in 1952.

The TVLR was never the most convenient of lines. It took well over an hour to travel the 19m to Oswestry, and the valley stations were sited generally too far from the centres of population. But the railway was a godsend to the quarries, especially to the Craig Rhiwarth workings above the village, which had always had problems in getting the slate down to Llangynog and then out of the valley.

It is possible to clamber up to the workings and to obtain some idea of the difficulties involved. Walk past the garage and on to the lane to the right just beyond it. After a few yards you can see the wharf where the slate was loaded on to wagons. This is also the bottom of the incline where loads were wound down, and the trackbed can be clearly seen descending steeply from the hillside; the remains of the winding gear are still there at the top.

4½
**

The starting point of the walk is the old sledge track which can be seen traversing the hill diagonally from the wharf. It starts as a grassy path, but soon becomes bedded with loose slate. It was down this track that sledges loaded with slate were perilously guided by men who got 2d for each descent and return. You eventually emerge on to the first level, which extends to the top of the incline. The way up to the second level is clear, and this is probably the most interesting section, with tunnel entries and bits of abandoned machinery. A difficult climb over loose slate brings

you to the third and oldest level, and from here it is a short distance to a plateau which leads gently to the summit, marked by a small cairn. This is the site of a large Iron Age village, and many hut circles can be seen around the cairn; if you walk down the other side you come across the remains of a dry stone wall dating from the same period. From here the way off is due west (there is no perceptible path) down to the Llangynog-Bala road.

7½
*

An easier walk along quiet lanes leads to the remote church of Pennant Melangell. (Warning — if you want to look inside it ask at the Post Office for the key.) The walk starts at the south end of the village, where you came in. Cross the river bridge and immediately turn right along a lane which follows the Tanat for about 2½m before crossing it to bring you to the church. The legend has it that an Irish princess named Monacella (Melangell) lived as a hermit in this area. Brochwel, Prince of Powys, was hunting here one day when a hare that he was chasing took refuge in the folds of Monacella's gown. The hounds ran away, and the event so impressed the Prince that he helped Monacella to establish an abbey here. The present church dates from the twelfth century and was extensively restored in the 1890s. The main features of interest are a fifteenth-century rood screen, now removed to the gallery, and a 1958 reconstruction of the saint's shrine, pieced together from the original fragments.

4
**

From the rear of the churchyard you can see a gushing waterfall at the extreme head of the valley. It can be reached by continuing along the road past the church to the point where it peters out and then taking a path to the left (GR 020270). For those returning directly, follow the lane back and take

Pennant Melangell Church, Tanat Valley

the left fork after about half a mile. This leads back on the other side of the river and comes out in the middle of the village.

Llangynog is still virtually unknown in spite of its chalets and caravan sites. No doubt it is only a matter of time before its industrial history is enshrined in commercial exhibitions and 'show caverns', but at the moment it can be walked over free of charge, and a detailed tour provides a fascinating insight into a hectic and often tragic past.

There was tragedy of a different kind in the creation of Lake Vyrnwy, reached by way of a turning at Penybontfawr. After the open mountain ranges of the Tanat Valley you are suddenly plunged into a heavily-forested area that casts something of a chill. Just before arriving at the dam you pass through Llanwyddyn, a village built in the 1890s to rehouse the inhabitants of the original Llanwyddyn, which now lies at the bottom of the lake.

The plan to flood the Vyrnwy valley in order to supply Liverpool with water was first mooted in 1865. It was an obvious choice, with many feeder streams, a 'bottleneck' at one end, and a bar of rock to make an ideal foundation for a dam. The necessary Act of Parliament was passed in 1880, and eight years later the dam was complete. The reservoir took a year to fill, but, with 68m of piping to instal, the first Welsh water did not reach Liverpool until

The Straining Tower, Lake Vyrnwy

1892. In the meantime the old village was dismantled and the residents moved, in an operation which today would no doubt inspire outraged protest.

Whatever the rights and wrongs of it all, the lake is there today, pumping its daily 45 million gallons. It has a somewhat gloomy, Scandinavian appearance — a featureless expanse of water with forestry plantations extending right to the shores. A 'gothic' tower, reminiscent of a Hollywood medieval castle, stands out from the bank near the dam; this is the 'straining tower' — the plug-hole in fact, where the water starts on its way to Liverpool.

The Severn-Trent Water Authority publish various pamphlets extolling the beauty of the lake and the variety of its wild-life, and have opened a Visitor Centre at the western end of the dam. Another recent feature is a nature trail through the nearby Craig Garth Bwlch area below the dam. It is possible to do a complete 11m circuit of the lake, but it has to be said that it lacks excitement, in spite of the best efforts of the commentary pamphlet available at the Centre.

The road back from the dam divides after a mile, and by taking the B4393 you can take in the small town of Llanfyllin, which became a borough in 1293. It is one of only two Welsh boroughs — Welshpool is the other — to receive charters from native Welsh princes. Although the older part of the town spreads itself on each side of the main road, it still has the intimate atmosphere of a close-knit community.

Eminent musicians gather in July each year for a festival which attracts wide interest, and the town prides itself on its floral decorations — the grounds of Bodfach Hall, now a hotel, are a mecca for gardening enthusiasts during May when the rhododendrons and azaleas are in bloom.

The parish church is well worth seeing as a rare example of an eighteenth-century church, but rather more famous in Welsh history is the Pendref Congregational Chapel. Nonconformist worship started here in 1640, although the present building dates from 1717, and it was here that the legendary Ann Griffiths was converted in 1796. Hers was a romantic story. She was born a few miles away and died at the age of 29 after writing over seventy hymns, which survived only because her servant was later able to recite them from memory.

Llanfyllin has a fine mixture of domestic architecture, but two houses in the centre stand out — the Georgian manor house and the Hall, which was built in 1599 but 'adapted' out of recognition in the early nineteenth century. A number of French prisoners were lodged in the town during the Napoleonic Wars, and one officer left a permanent memorial in the form of wall paintings, which can still be seen in the Council House.

The road back to Oswestry follows the river Cain (there is a river Abel to the south). Two miles out of the town you turn left, pass through the rather featureless village of Llansantffraid and eventually reach the extensive quarrying area of Llanyblodwel and Porthywaen. A short diversion to Llanyblodwel church is recommended in order to see the exotically-painted interior. Just before Llynclys you pass over the only surviving section of the complex network of railway lines laid in this area during the railway mania of the nineteenth century; it is used by an occasional train collecting ballast from a nearby quarry.

Just past the railway on your right is a lay-by and a signpost for Turner's Lane. This is a good starting point for a walk over the Llynclys and Llanymynech hills. In the old days Llynclys Hill was a favourite picnic spot for Oswestry people, who were able to get a cheap excursion ticket on the train. On reaching the end of Turner's Lane, it is best to walk along the north side of the hill with its views of the Tanat Valley. You pass over the golf course and reach the heavily-quarried Llanymynech Hill. This area has been mined ever since the Romans dug for lead; their shafts and tunnels are still evident, and in 1965 a group of schoolboys found a hoard of Roman silver coins in one of them.

The limestone quarries closed down around 1900, but in their time they stimulated an enormous amount of local industrial activity, including the railway system already mentioned and the Montgomery canal.

If a considerate friend has driven the car round from Llynclys, you can descend to Llanymynech village, using a section of the Offa's Dyke path. One of the main features of interest is the church, built in 1845 in a rare neo-Norman style and dedicated to St Agatha. Its clock was designed by a local inventor. Equally notable is the Lion, a pub with the border running through it, leading to complications when the former county of Montgomeryshire was ' dry' on Sundays.

Llanymynech is the last stop on this tour, but in another chapter we shall go south along the main road (much of which is a causeway through the flood plain) towards Welshpool and the heartland of mid-Wales.

2 North West Shropshire

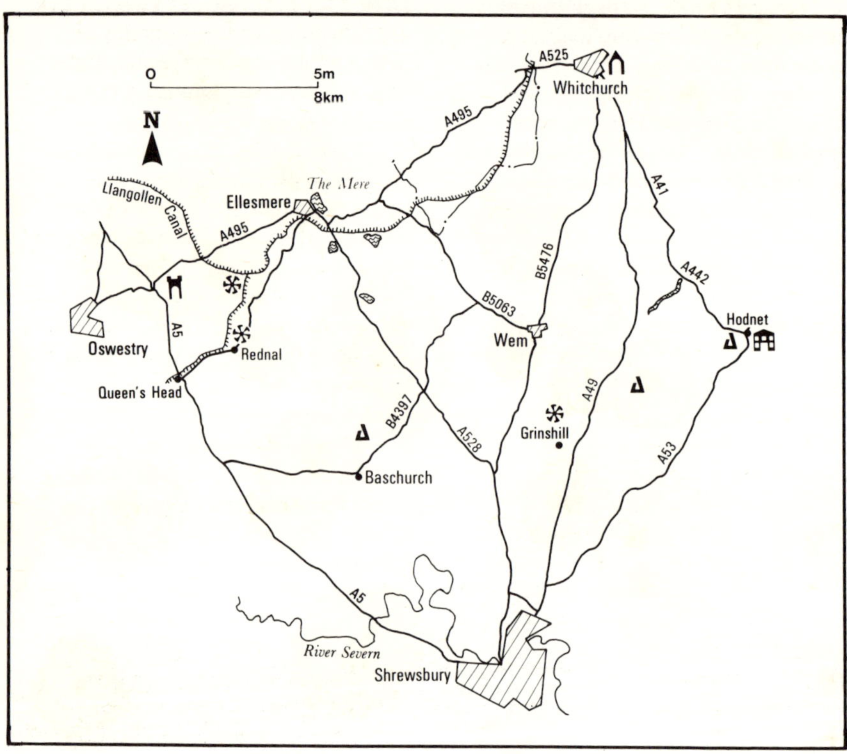

The border areas explored so far have obvious appeal to the visitor — an embattled past, links with early industry, the sharp contrast of mountains and valleys, the signs of man's attempts to force progress on to difficult terrain.

The North Shropshire landscape comes as a complete contrast. It is a pastoral plain, where the inhabitants have co-operated with nature to produce a rich agricultural economy. It is sometimes called 'the black and white country', and the reason is clear as you pass millions of pounds' worth of Friesian cows surrounding hundreds of half-timbered buildings (many of them genuine).

Not an area, then, of dramatic landscape, but there is plenty of that elsewhere in the border country; what North Shropshire offers is tranquillity and a long history of stable community life.

Ellesmere is ten miles from Oswestry, and to reach it you leave on the A495, passing on the left the huge garrison area of Park Hall, now being restored to civilian use. The black and white lodge by the roadside gives some idea of what the original Park Hall looked like before it was burnt down.

Whittington is a mellow village with the misfortune to have the A5 running through the middle of it. You turn left at the junction, then almost immediately right at the church. Between the two turns there is the unusual sight of a castle at ground level, a reminder that this was once marshland and that Whittington guarded one of the few feasible routes through it. The most striking features of this thirteenth-century structure are the moat and the fine twin-towered gateway; the surprise on the other side of the gate is the tiny half-timbered house built against the wall. (One of the gatehouses is in use as a craft shop.) The restoration of the castle dates only from 1967, and it revealed a good deal that had been hidden, but came too late to prevent much of the original stone disappearing into local houses and roads.

The fact that the castle was held for 300 years by the Fitzwarine family has given rise to the belief that the village was the birthplace of Dick Whittington, who got a job with an Alderman Fitzwarren when he went to London. A better-authenticated local association is with William Walsham How, the prolific contributor to 'Hymns Ancient and Modern', who was Rector here for 28 years. Most of his hymns have been

Castle gatehouse, Whittington

consigned to obscurity, but he will not share that fate while congregations continue to sing his masterpiece 'For all the saints who from their labours rest'.

Having turned at the church and passed through the village, you will notice an impressive park entrance on the right. This leads to Halston Hall (not open to the public), which was the home of the Mytton family. Thomas Mytton was one of Cromwell's most trusted generals, but it was the black sheep of the family who became more famous locally. 'Mad Jack' Mytton was one of the great Shropshire eccentrics, a hard-riding and hard-drinking squire of the early nineteenth century who ended his life at the age of 38 in a debtor's prison. He managed to cram a good deal of zestful living into his short span. Many of his supposed exploits as a horseman verge on fantasy, but it is well known that he would ride the length of the county and back in a single day in order to get in a few hours' hunting with his favourite Staffordshire pack. The outstanding feature of Halston Hall itself is the family church, one of only two timber-framed churches in Shropshire (the other is at Melverley).

A mile further on is Welsh Frankton, which used to be important as the junction of the Shropshire Union Canal and its Montgomery branch. A breach in 1936, never repaired, put an end to traffic on the branch, although volunteer restoration work is now going on. As it happens, Welsh Frankton has regained some of its former status among canal users through the development of a marina, which can be seen on the left as you approach the village. The old junction is reached by turning right to Lower Frankton.

Ellesmere announces itself as 'Shropshire's Lake District'. Justified or not, the sign is the first indication of those characteristic features of North Shropshire — the Meres and Mosses.

They are what geologists call a recent phenomenon, which means that they go back no further than the last Ice Age. As the ice melted, it left behind a mass of glacial debris, and, at those points where the ice paused in its retreat, the debris formed into hillocks and dips. The hollows filled with water like huge puddles without the help of feeder streams, and it is this that distinguishes a mere from a lake. Ellesmere has eight notable examples in its vicinity, including the largest, which gives the town its name. Originally there were many more, but they have silted up or become full of vegetation, and large marshy areas of this kind, called mosses, are a prominent feature further east.

Before exploring the meres it is worth looking at Ellesmere itself. Its narrow streets follow no detectable pattern, and its architecture is a mixture of half-timber and mellow eighteenth and nineteenth-century styles. It has been a small agricultural town and later an important canal centre. The large wharf area still has atmosphere — a freshly-painted notice on a warehouse proclaims the Shropshire Union Canal Co as General Carriers to Liverpool, Manchester, Chester and North Wales — but the activity nowadays is centred on holiday narrow boats and cabin cruisers.

Prominent in the Square is the curiously-designed Town Hall with its overhanging pediment. The most attractive buildings, however, lie towards the mere and especially around the church, which stands on a steep hill. Its finest feature is a south chapel with a superb fifteenth-century carved oak ceiling; also of interest is the sixteenth-century altar tomb of Sir Francis Kynaston and his wife — Sir Francis

Chirk Castle gates, near Llangollen

Chirk Aqueduct, Llangollen Canal

Tanat Valley in the Berwyns

Berwyn Mountains

Derelict locks, now under repair, at the junction of the Shropshire Union and Montgomery canals, Welsh Frankton

PLACES OF INTEREST IN AND AROUND ELLESMERE

The Wharf
Former depot of Shropshire Union, now a canal basin popular with pleasure craft in summer.

The Mere
Lake with wide variety of bird life. Visitor Centre with information about natural history and geology of meres.

Cremorne Gardens, by the Mere below church
Children's playground, lakeside walk, boats for hire, tennis courts etc.

Colemere and White Mere, south-east of Ellesmere
Both these lakes have sailing clubs.

Canal at Welsh Frankton, 4m west of Ellesmere on A495
Canal boat marina (boats for hire) and junction locks of old Montgomery canal, now being restored.

Rednal and Queen's Head, 7m south-west of Ellesmere
Interesting canal features; wharves, warehouses etc.

Stanwardine Hall, on minor road off A528 south of Cockshutt (5m south-east of Ellesmere)
3-storey Elizabethan mansion, now used as farmhouse. Open by appointment only (Cockshutt 212).

The Mere, Ellesmere

was cup-bearer to Elizabeth I.

As you emerge from the confined spaces of the town, the mere looks immense. It does, in fact, cover nearly 120 acres, and, apart from two small artificial islands, is an unbroken sheet of water. Visitors are attracted particularly by the plentiful bird life, much of which parades on the shore when there is the prospect of food. Coots, moorhens, swans, various species of duck and the large Canada geese are usually in evidence, and the shyer birds such as herons and cormorants can sometimes be seen from the 'hide' at the Visitor Centre.

At the town end of the mere are the attractive Cremorne Gardens, with sporting facilities, play areas for children and boats for hire in the summer. The footpath through the gardens will take you to the opposite side of the mere, although it is not possible to make the complete circuit.

The botanist or ornithologist will probably want to explore at least part of the area on foot, and various easy walks are possible. About a mile from the town, where the A495 to Whitchurch branches from the A528 there is a small roadside parking area. A footpath leads from here down to the canal towpath, and by turning left you quickly reach Blake Mere, which is comparatively undisturbed and has a brooding air. Walk under the next canal bridge, numbered 56, and after a short distance you will see some rusting hulks moored in a basin on the far side of the canal. They are bulk-cargo narrow boats, a reminder of former commercial prosperity and a sad contrast to the brightly-painted holiday craft that pass at regular intervals in the summer, navigated with various degrees of skill or incipient panic.

8½
*

At bridge 55 cross the canal and follow the path to Colemere, past a well-restored black and white cottage. Colemere has a sailing club and is being developed into a recreational area, including a circuit path. It may be preferable to walk along the south side of the mere to Colemere village and then take the minor road back towards Ellesmere; this will bring you to White Mere, home of the Shropshire Sailing Club. From here it is necessary to walk back along the main road (the traffic is light) to your starting point.

The shorter alternative is to return to bridge 55 and follow the track beyond the bridge to a crossroads, where you turn left to reach Newton Mere. A track and path off to the left takes you to bridge 56 and the towpath where you started.

Crose Mere and Sweat Mere lie about two miles south of the main group and are difficult to reach, being within private land; in any case the official policy is to preserve them as sites of scientific interest. The forested area next to them is Whettal Moss, once a mere and now taken over by vegetation.

Back in the car the route is now the A495 towards Whitchurch, and very soon you reach the village of Welshampton, unremarkable except for its small yellow church with a patterned tile roof. There is an unexpected feature here — one of the graves is that of Moshueshue, son of a Basuto chief, who came to England to study at a missionary college and died while staying in the village. He is also commemorated in a stained glass window.

There is now an uneventful drive to Whitchurch, described later in the chapter. If you have more time to spare, you may like to sample the area south of Ellesmere by turning on to the B5063 at Welshampton (signposted Wem). What the countryside lacks in dramatic impact, it makes up for in curiosities; for example, about 4 miles from Welshampton is a turning left for the village of Newtown, which has one of the rare churches dedicated to Charles I. During the Commonwealth, several local royalists converted a private house into a church and dedicated it to the former King, and the present Victorian church has retained the dedication, going so far as to display pictures of Charles I's execution.

About a mile later, turn right on to the B4397 to reach Loppington, which has the characteristic local mixture of brick and timber-framed houses and a bull-baiting ring, reputed to have been used last in 1835. There are echoes of the Civil War here, too, because Loppington church was garrisoned by Parliamentary forces and successfully stormed by Royalist troops. Several of Loppington's houses are of architectural interest, as is Burlton Grange a mile further on — it is late-Victorian Tudor and has a cruck-framed cottage nearby.

Black-and-white houses are such a feature of the border that the style has become an accepted form of exterior decoration. At Cockshutt two houses, Shade Oak and Wycherley Hall, exemplify the custom of painting brickwork as imitation half-timber. Connoisseurs of architecture will also appreciate the eighteenth-century church at nearby Petton, which has box pews facing inwards across an aisle and a fine Jacobean pulpit.

The B4397 now leads into Baschurch, a nondescript half-town, half-village with an old centre but extensive modern housing which has altered its character. The Shropshire Conservation Trust have established a nature trail at Merrington Green, an area of common land to the east of Baschurch. You reach it by taking the Shrewsbury road out of Baschurch and turning left soon after passing the Walford Agricultural College. Merrington Green has had a colourful history; at one time it was notorious for its gipsy encampments, and during the second World War it accommodated a US Army camp. Now its 30 acres are reverting from pasture to scrub and heathland. The start of the trail is at the lane junction GR 465209.

On the other side of Baschurch is the Berth (GR 429237), a double earthwork with a linking causeway that has puzzled archaeologists for a long time. It is one of the few Iron Age forts in the border area not built on a hill, and no doubt relied for defence on a moat and the surrounding marshland. There is evidence that it was a place of considerable importance — it is mentioned in a Welsh sixth-century poem as the site of a decisive battle between the Saxons and the army of Powys — and some scholars have even identified it as Pengwern, the legendary capital of Powys.

Ruyton-XI-Towns has retained more character than Baschurch. It gets its curious name from the fact that in the twelfth century eleven townships were united in the one manor. Today it is a long, right-angled village, extending along a ridge and down a steep hill and revealing a good deal of the red sandstone building material so common in this part of Shropshire. The big blocks used must have made house-building a rapid process. The church, substantially Norman, is built in this material, and there are some sketchy remains of a castle nearby. Boreatton Park to the north, now an adventure holiday centre, is of some historical interest because it was here that Agnes Hunt founded the hospital that was later to be moved to

Oswestry to become the internationally-known Orthopaedic Hospital.

As you move out of Ruyton you pass the nineteenth-century 'castle' known as Ruyton Towers and reach the A5, which is the western boundary of this tour. West Felton appears at first to be a straggle of buildings on the main road, but the village proper is a quarter of a mile to the west, and is a pleasant cluster of church, houses and trees. As at Ruyton, there is a castle site next to the church.

The route is now back to Ellesmere by the back door. A mile from West Felton is Queen's Head, and a right turn here on to a minor road (signposted Rednal) will take you through a rather desolate stretch of low-lying ground. You will notice the forlorn-looking stretch of canal following the dead-straight road; it is part of the section of the Montgomery canal which starts at Welsh Frankton and is now undergoing restoration. It is difficult to believe that this length once bustled with commercial life, not only at the important junction with the A5, but also a mile further towards Rednal, where the Shrewsbury-Chester railway line crosses.

The dignified buildings on the right soon after Tetchill are those of the public school, Ellesmere College, and a little further on you cross the main Shropshire Union Canal at the point where an arm branches to Ellesmere wharf. Finally a perilously narrow road decants you back into the town.

After all this meandering in country lanes, Whitchurch seems like a major metropolis. As you enter it, you need to keep a sharp lookout for signs to the town centre, otherwise the efficient ring road system will land you on the other side, having seen nothing but the dull villas and bungalows that surround the older part of the town. What you find when you finally break in is a handsome town with a harmonious blend of architecture, dominated by the tall tower of St Alkmund's church.

The original church here was reputedly founded by King Alfred's daughter, who dedicated it to her ancestor Alkmund. It was replaced at an unknown date by a limestone structure that presumably gave the town its name, and this in turn gave place to a large church, possibly in the fourteenth century. This fell down in 1711. The present sandstone building was then erected in elegant eighteenth-century style. The effect was somewhat spoilt by Victorian additions, particularly the stained glass which has made the east end of the church far gloomier than it was ever intended to be.

The most famous feature of the church is the tomb of John Talbot, Earl of Shrewsbury, who was born near Whitchurch and died after the battle of Bordeaux in 1453. There is a certain amount of human interest in Talbot's death because he was first buried in France, and not until fifty years later were his bones and heart brought home by his grandson for re-burial at Whitchurch. The heart now lies under the porch, but the bones, which were originally placed in the tomb, were disturbed during restoration work in 1874. They were found to be in a box, with each bone wrapped in cloth, but the remarkable thing was that a family of mummified mice were found in the skull, having found their way in through the fatal gash. Photographs of the bones

Bargates, Whitchurch

before re-interment can be seen at the tomb.

On the opposite side of the church behind the organ is the effigy of another Talbot — Sir John, who founded the town's grammar school in 1550. The general impression of the church is of typical eighteenth-century elegance, with tall columns, generous windows and an air of spaciousness. There is some good woodwork, too, in the organ case and the vestry door at the west end.

Almost next door to the church, at the bottom of Bargates, is the building which last housed the grammar school. It is a distinguished, mid-Victorian building in appropriate Elizabethan style — very different from the modern complex on the outskirts of the town which the present comprehensive school occupies. Between the old school and the church, and looking slightly the worse for wear, are the Higginson Almshouses. They are, in fact, a set of Georgian cottages, and very attractive too, especially with the charming infants' school of 1708.

The local council publishes a 'town trail', giving purpose to a stroll around a town that needs to be walked in, in order to appreciate its homely atmosphere and relaxed pace. The Trail points out two features not to be missed — the superb cast-iron shopfront that faces you as you emerge from the Civic Centre after buying the pamphlet, and the Alexandra Stables at the back of the same building. It was once the Alexandra Hotel, and the stables had room for over eighty horses in the days when farmers rode to market.

If you have the time, walk down Watergate Street into the suburb of Dodington, once the 'smart' district of Whitchurch. There are several good timber-framed houses along here, but the outstanding buildings are the large Mansion House and the former Congregational Chapel, now being turned into a leisure centre. The almshouses opposite date from the 1820s.

The area to the south-west of Whitchurch will probably appeal most to anyone interested in ecology or plant life. It is dominated by Fenn's Moss, the extensive peat bog, and by the extraordinary settlement called Whixall, which is not so much a village as a scattered collection of houses lining an intricate network of lanes. (An Ordnance Survey map is strongly advised.) The shortest route is back on the Ellesmere Road; after turning left at Redbrook take the minor road about a mile after, signposted Whixall. As you approach the canal you see to the left a counterweighted lifting bridge, a rare feature in these parts.

The absence of signposts now becomes a problem, and the map will be needed in order to travel due south to the canal bridge near Moss Cottages. It is best to walk from here along the towpath, from which tracks lead out into the Moss itself. Peat is still cut here, for horticultural use rather than as fuel.

A circular walk is possible by turning left where the canal divides (GR 489353), taking the track to Moss Farm, crossing the canal and taking either of the two tracks which lead off to the right. They converge by a wood, and half a mile later reach a T-junction. Turn right, keeping the wood on your right, go under the canal and then follow a path which brings you after half a mile to the trackbed of the old Oswestry-Whitchurch line. It runs dead straight for three miles across the Moss and posed a severe technical problem for the engineers, who solved it by laying the track on a brushwood raft sunk into the peat. Continue walking, ignoring tracks to the left, and make for the corner of the conifer wood (GR 487377). At the next corner of the wood a track leads to Lodge Farm and continues to a featureless cross roads. Turn right here and walk down the mile of straight track to Moss Cottages and your starting point.

Whitchurch may be grander than Wem and may boast the birthplace of the composer Edward German, but Wem can claim more famous associations. William Hazlitt, the essayist and critic, lived here in his youth at a house in Noble Street — in fact his first published words were written here in the form of a letter to the Shrewsbury Chronicle. Another resident for a time was William Henry Betty, who had an extraordinary career as a child actor at the end of the eighteenth century. He became such a cult figure in London that on one occasion the House of Commons was adjourned so that William Pitt could attend one of his performances, but by the time he arrived in Wem his celebrity days were over and he was a has-been in his forties. Another native of the town was John Astley, who became famous as a society portrait painter. The most famous local resident, however, was the first Baron Wem, who bought the title in 1685, the year in which he was achieving notoriety in the West Country as Judge Jeffries, sent to punish supporters of the Monmouth rebellion. His house, Lowe Hall, is a mile or so to the north-west.

There is nothing remarkable about Wem itself, unless it is the quality of its famous beer. Like all these North Shropshire towns it is designed for plain living and working, and, like Oswestry, it suffered a fire which deprived it of most of its older buildings. Nowadays the High Street is dominated by the church, approached through an

PLACES OF INTEREST IN AND AROUND WHITCHURCH

St Alkmund's Church
Good example of early eighteenth-century church, but interior spoilt at west end by Victorian additions. Notable tomb of Sir John Talbot.

Old Grammar School and Almshouses, in Bargates, next to the church

Alexandra Stables, Newtown Road
Interesting hotel stable block, formerly accommodating 80 horses.

Civic Centre, High Street
Sports Hall, Market Hall, centre for entertainment of all kinds.

Shropshire Arts and Crafts Centre, Brownlow Street
Building is interesting early fire station. Shropshire-made crafts on sale. Art and craft materials.

Cholmondeley Castle, 6m north-west on A49
Ornamental gardens, lakeside picnic area, rare breeds of farm animal, tearoom, shop etc. Private chapel can be visited.

Black Prince Marina, canal at Whixall, off A49 6m south of Whitchurch
Daily boat hire.

Grindley Brook Locks, on Shropshire Union by side of A41, 2m north of Whitchurch
Very busy in summer months.

impressive eighteenth-century gateway.
The tower is fourteenth-century, but the
remainder is mainly the result of
Victorian restoration. This included a
roomy gallery on three sides of the nave,
supported by iron pillars, and a
wrought-iron pulpit.

Wem is the centre of some interesting
countryside, including the famous
Grinshill quarries, which from Roman
times to the present century provided the
sandstone for distinguished buildings in
many part of England. Many of the
quarrymen lived in Wem, and it is
possible to follow the path which they
trod to work.

The walk is clearly marked on the
Ordnance Survey map, leaving the
B5476 at Oaklands, just to the south of
Wem. It crosses to Tilley Green, passes
Trench Hall and then runs clear for a
mile before meeting a track. Turn right
at the track, then left after a few hundred
yards on to another path past a pond.
This path crosses the road on the
outskirts of Clive and goes up the field
to a cinder track. Turn right and then
left to reach the top of Grinshill.

This is a notable area for wildlife
observation, and part of it has been
taken into the care of the Shropshire
Conservation Trust, which has
established a nature trail in Corbet
Wood on the eastern side of the hill. The
wood contains a quarry face where some
caution is necessary. The trail is
accessible by car from Clive, where a
leaflet is usually available from the Post
Office. Clive Hall, incidentally, was the
birthplace of the Restoration dramatist
William Wycherley, who found success
in London but spent many years of his
life in a debtor's prison. Grinshill is a
fascinating area, of particular interest to
the naturalist or industrial archaeologist,
but equally attractive as a place for a
picnic or a leisurely stroll.

Another easy walk from Wem will
take you to Edstaston, which is worth a
visit whether you walk or not, because of
the medieval wall-paintings in the
church, the wharf and warehouses by the
canal and a bridge by Thomas Telford.
Again the walk is clear on the map,
leaving Wem at the cemetery on the
northern edge of the town and heading
straight to Highfields. Turning right
here along the road to the next T-
junction, pass through the gate near the
signpost. Edstaston church soon
becomes visible and the path comes out
close to it.

The Whitchurch — Shrewsbury road
through Wem is technically the eastern
limit of the area covered by this book,
but it would be unfortunate to ignore the
area due east of Wem. Hodnet has
become famous largely because of
Hodnet Hall Gardens — 60 acres of
superb landscaping which can fill a
whole day for the enthusiastic gardener.
It was the remarkable achievement of
the late Brigadier Heber-Percy, who
spent thirty years transforming an
unpromising wilderness. The neo-
Elizabethan house, though not open,
can be admired from the outside. The
tea-room, surprisingly, is in the middle
of a museum of taxidermy.

There are several attractive half-
timbered houses in Hodnet, and the
large church contains some impressive
memorials to local families. The
Norman door was retained during
nineteenth-century restoration.

Spectacular in quite a different way is
Hawkstone Park, close by to the north-
west. Reputedly the first stately home to
be opened to the public (and not open
now, unfortunately) it was laid out in the
eighteenth-century to suit the taste of the
time for ruins, lakes and romantic
grottoes. It was the estate of a branch of
the Hill family, and the park contains an

obelisk with a statue of Sir Rowland
Hill, Lord Mayor of London in 1555.
The most impressive feature is probably
Grotto Hill, where old mines were
exploited in the landscaping. Part of the
estate is now occupied by an attractive
Georgian hotel and a golf course.

The southern boundary of
Hawkestone Park is a sandstone

escarpment, thickly wooded, and on its
edge is a massive Iron Age fort with
three ramparts. Known as Bury Walls, it
has been the subject of much
speculation, and it is believed that it may
once have been a major settlement.
Certainly its 20 acres and elaborate
sandstone walls point to something
more than a purely military post. It may
have been used by the Romans in
connection with the army post of
Rutunium, which may have been in the
same neighbourhood. As at Old
Oswestry and The Berth, systematic
excavation has yet to take place.

The nearby A49 takes you direct to
Shrewsbury, but anyone who has ever
read Shakespeare's 'Henry IV Part One'
will want to stop a mile or so before the
outskirts of the town in order to see the
site of the battle of Shrewsbury. It was a
notable victory for Henry in 1403
against the rebel nobles who were
threatening the country's stability, and
saw the death of the colourful 'Harry
Hotspur', son of the Earl of
Northumberland. (There were so many
rumours that he had escaped alive that
his body was placed at the High Cross in
Shrewsbury for all to see.) After the
battle Henry decided to build a
memorial church on the site and to
found a college of priests to serve it.

Battlefield church is still there. You
reach it by means of a right turn not
signposted from the north, about two
miles after the village of Hadnall. It has
a distinguished interior on the collegiate
pattern, with a small nave and large
chancel. The atmosphere is austere and
spacious, and the medieval air is
reinforced by the gargoyles representing
knights and the coats of arms of those
who fought with the King in the battle.

3 Shrewsbury, Church Stretton and the Clun Forest

The old town of Shrewsbury was built in a perfect defensive position, almost completely surrounded by a huge loop of the river Severn, which fails by a few hundred yards to complete the circle. The river forms a natural moat, and the castle dominates the narrow neck of land that once provided the only 'dry' access.

Shrewsbury used to announce itself modestly on its road signs as 'a medieval town', and although it is full of traffic

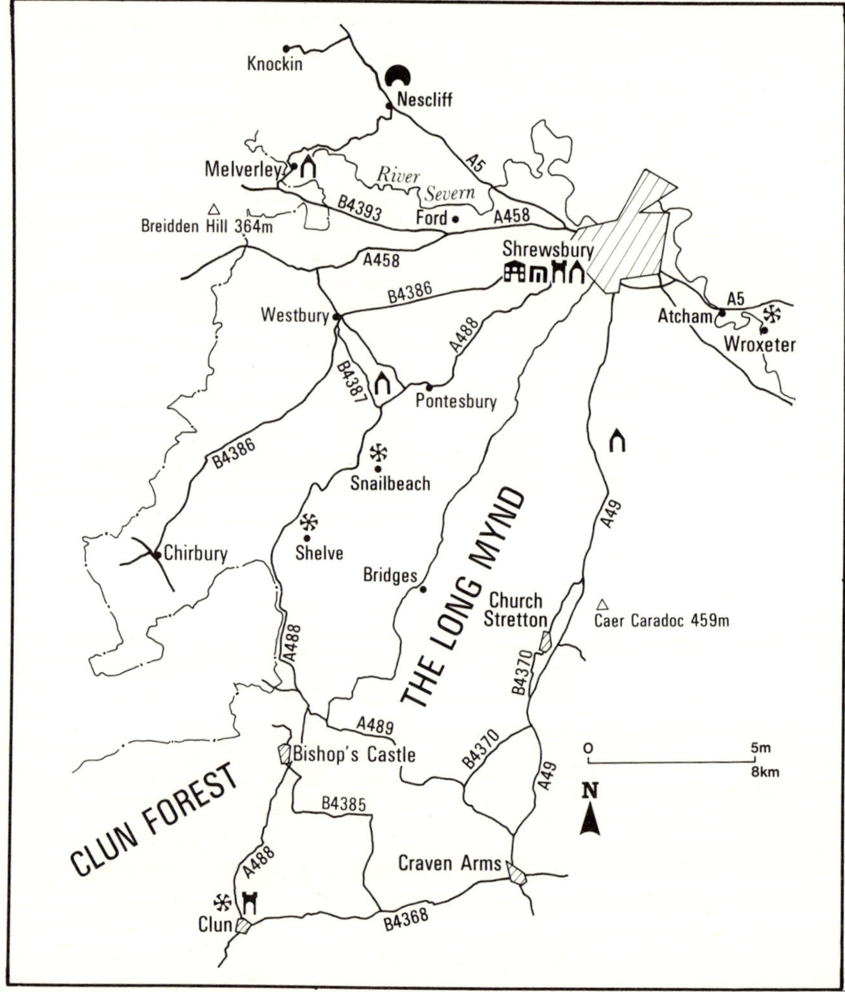

and has spread well beyond its original boundaries, the oldest quarter preserves the medieval ground plan, and there are half-timbered buildings wherever you look. You can get away from the traffic, too, in dozens of narrow alleyways or 'shuts'. The town has over a thousand listed buildings, and many of the oldest are far from being museum pieces. It comes as a surprise to find 'Bubbles — Hair Stylist' or the Empire cinema occupying fine Tudor houses, and when Boots built a new store the facade was suspended in position while a completely new structure went up behind it. This policy of letting old buildings go on earning their living has paid off handsomely.

The area within the river loop is not extensive and can be inspected in the course of a morning's stroll. The magnificent railway station below the castle is a good place to start; built on the lines of a venerable Oxford college it is a fitting monument to past railway glories. By walking up the steep Castle Gates and turning left into an alley called The Dana it is possible to cross the railway by a footbridge. You emerge opposite the prison, but if you go down the hill to the left you come to the Howard Street Warehouse, now being converted into a theatre. Built in 1835, it is a fine example of a functional building designed on classical lines. The interior, if you can see it, is far more impressive than the outside.

The castle itself dates from the eleventh century, but was greatly restored by Thomas Telford at the end of the eighteenth century and is now a rather gracious building doubling as a museum. Immediately opposite is the public library, housed in what was Shrewsbury School until the school moved across the river in 1882. In front the statue of Charles Darwin is a reminder of the school's most famous old boy, born in the suburb of Frankwell just across the Welsh Bridge. Adjoining the castle is Castle Gates House, the first of many superb timber-framed buildings.

Castle Street meets the pedestrianised Pride Hill, and the traffic proceeds round into St Mary's Street. This area has a cluster of buildings of great interest. It gets its name from St Mary's church, with its 200-foot spire and magnificent stained glass. Curiously enough, very little of this famous glass was designed for St Mary's. The Jesse window in the chancel was originally at St Chad's, while much of the rest is French or German, either bought by a mid-nineteenth-century incumbent or donated to him. Flemish work is also well represented. The fine nave roof and graceful arcades are only the more obvious features of a church that makes a long visit rewarding.

Beyond the church is the former Royal Infirmary, now being converted for other uses but noted in its time for being one of Britain's earliest major hospital buildings. A lane opposite St Mary's leads to an oasis containing two churches, St Alkmund's (late eighteenth century) and St Julian's, which has been de-consecrated and is now a crafts centre. Also here is the group of fifteenth and sixteenth-century buildings known as Bear Steps, which decayed picturesquely until 1968, when the Shrewsbury Civic Society started a programme of renovation. There are further architectural riches in nearby Butcher Row.

St Mary's Street continues as Dogpole, where the outstanding building is the Guildhall, erected by the Earl of Bradford at the end of the seventeenth century after he had moved his own house from this site nearer the

Bear Steps, Shrewsbury

castle. This sort of operation was not uncommon — timber-framed buildings were pre-fabricated in the first place, and were easy to dismantle and re-erect.

Dogpole in turn becomes Wyle Cop — various attempts have been made to explain Shrewsbury's extraordinary street names — and winds downhill to the English Bridge. Dominating the hill is the Lion Hotel, for long the meeting-place of county society. It was here that a crowd used to gather to watch the London stagecoach arrive; Paderewski performed here and Dickens was one of many celebrities who stayed here. Now owned by a hotel chain, it remains an impressive building.

You now cross the English Bridge and have a choice of three very different attractions. To the left is the incongruously-named Gay Meadow, the home of Shrewsbury Town Football Club. To the right, along Coleham Head, is the old pumping station, now open as a museum for engineering enthusiasts. Straight ahead is the Abbey Church, part of the Benedictine monastery founded by Earl Roger of Montgomery in about 1080; he was to die there in 1094, three days after entering it as a monk. The church survived the destruction of the rest of the monastery because it had become a place of public worship.

Although the interior is a mixture of many styles and dates, the over-riding impression is of massive Norman strength. There is a curious collection of sculptured figures at the west end of the nave, most of them discarded by other churches, and other distinctive features are a font fashioned from the base of a pillar and the remains of the shrine of St Winifred. The east end of the church is the result of unusually sensitive Victorian restoration.

Until 1836 part of the monastery's refectory survived to the south of the church, but in that year Telford drove his Holyhead road through the ruins, leaving the refectory pulpit isolated on the other side. It still stands there today — a beautiful survival at odds with its surroundings.

After so much antiquity it is a change to return across the bridge, ignore Wyle Cop on the right and continue straight on to reach the town walls. You now enter a district of Georgian and Victorian elegance, particularly in the streets leading off the Walls, because this was one of the earliest areas of clearance and re-development. The impressive Roman Catholic Cathedral is along here on the right. It was built in 1856 from a design by Edward Pugin. The turning to the right soon after is Belmont, once the most fashionable street in town.

To the left is the river and an area now devoted largely to recreation. It includes

The Quarry, an attractive riverside park which has as its centrepiece the Dingle, a garden laid out by the most famous Parks Superintendent of all — Percy Thrower. In a commanding position above the Quarry is St Chad's church. Strictly speaking, it is New St Chad's, and its origins contain all the ingredients of a good short story.

Old St Chad's used to stand in Princess Street, off Belmont (the ruins are still there and worth a visit), and it was surveyed by Telford in 1788. He realised that a combination of faulty Norman building and undermining by burials beneath it had brought it to the point of collapse. He put in an urgent report to the authorities, only to have it scornfully rejected, but on July 9th the clock struck four and the tower tumbled down. Only the Lady Chapel survived. There could hardly have been a more elegant replacement. The new St Chad's finely-proportioned circular nave (the largest of its kind in Britain) has a superb gallery and beautiful decorations, and the exterior, with its portico and semi-detached tower, is equally grand.

There is a good view from here of Shrewsbury School, high up on the other side of the river. If the main building looks a little like a workhouse, the reason is that it was a workhouse until the school moved from its old buildings opposite the castle. It was built, in fact, in 1760 and had been used as a hospital, a woollen mill and a military prison.

The turning to the right just beyond St Chad's — Claremont Hill — brings you down into Barker Street, where Rowley's House stands marooned in an expanse of car park and bus station. It is one of Shrewsbury's most remarkable buildings, being a combination of a sixteenth-century timber-framed house and a stone-faced addition built in 1618. A recent face-lift and restoration has turned it into a fine museum, and among the exhibits are many items discovered at the site of the Roman town of Viroconium, to the east of Shrewsbury.

On returning to the centre of the town by way of Shoplatch you should turn right into High Street to look at the

St Chad's Church, Shrewsbury

Rowley's Mansion, Shrewsbury

Square. As you turn you pass Ireland's Mansion, the most spectacular example of timber-framed building in the town. Not surprisingly, it was a wool-merchant who built it in about 1575. The old Market Hall in the centre of the Square was erected a few years later, and its upper floor is still in use as the magistrates' court. Behind it is the Music Hall, the centre of Shrewsbury's musical and dramatic life since 1840, and behind that again, in College Street, is Clive House. Robert Clive, whose statue is in the Square, lived here for a time, and the house now accommodates a fine collection of china and porcelain as well as the regimental museum of the Queen's Dragoon Guards.

On the subject of military museums, Shrewsbury is probably unique in having five of them. In addition to Clive House there are the museums of the old Shropshire Light Infantry and the present Light Infantry Regiment at the Sir John Moore barracks in Copthorne Road. The Drill Hall at Coleham houses the Shropshire Volunteers collection, while Territorial House, in Sundorne Road, has a display of relics of the Shropshire Yeomanry and associated units.

One final, practical, point for the visitor who intends to spend a day in Shrewsbury; the main car park is in Frankwell, on the other side of the Welsh Bridge. A recently-installed footbridge over the river means that the vast parking area is only a short walk from the town centre.

The countryside to the east of

Shrewsbury is not really part of the border country, but two attractions in that direction cannot be ignored. The Roman town of Viroconium — the fourth largest in Britain — is reached by taking the A5 out of Shrewsbury and turning off on the Ironbridge road after Atcham. Ironbridge itself has become one large museum of industrial archaeology and can easily occupy a whole day.

Leaving Shrewsbury on the A5, you cross the Severn at Montford Bridge, which constitutes a dangerous kink in the road, owing to Telford's habit of building his bridges strictly at right-angles to the river, regardless of the approaches.

Shrawardine, a short distance along the river, had a brief surge of excitement in 1645, when the castle was besieged and captured by Parliamentary forces. Its main attraction today is its Pool, half a mile to the north, which has become a bird sanctuary. From the Pool the road goes on to rejoin the A5 at Nesscliffe, which shelters beneath a broad, wooded hill, made impressive by the flatness of the surrounding countryside. There is a hill fort at the top, and a cave reputed to have been the lair of Humphrey Kynaston, a legendary Robin Hood figure of the sixteenth century and the black sheep of a distinguished local family. It is still very much a local name — there are 86 Kynastons in the telephone directory, the vast majority living in the area west of Shrewsbury. The cave can be reached by a path almost opposite the point where you enter the village from Shrawardine.

Two miles further up the A5 you branch left for Knockin, approached through a fine avenue of mature trees. Nothing is left of the castle, but the village has some picturesque architecture and a Norman church in which a whole arcade has been incorporated into a later wall. A particularly striking window commemorates the son of a former incumbent who died in the First World War. Knockin's most unlikely feature stands in a field to the north-west — a giant radio telescope that looks as if it has been put out to grass.

If you have a good map and a competent navigator you can make your way from Knockin through Kinnerley and the maze of lanes beyond to Melverley, which stands close to the confluence of the Vyrnwy and Severn. Down a lane by the 'Tontine' pub is the fascinating black and white timber-framed church, beautifully maintained as befits a showpiece. The effect is one of rugged simplicity, especially inside, where a structure of massive, roughly-shaped timbers acts as a rood-screen. Although the church is no bigger than a large sitting-room, it has a tiny gallery reached by a flight of weirdly-distorted stairs. The Jacobean pulpit lends sophistication, but there is possibly no church where the sense of ancient local craftsmanship is so strong.

All this time, the scene has been dominated by the group of looming hills generally known as the Breiddens, although Breidden Hill is only the nearest of the three peaks. You drive towards them out of Melverley in order to cross the river and join the B4393 at Crew Green. The hills themselves are described in another chapter; for the moment you turn back towards Shrewsbury and very soon arrive at a road sign which seems to announce a village called Prince's Oak. In fact it simply draws attention to a tree enclosed in iron railings opposite the sign. It appears that when George IV was Prince of Wales he stayed at nearby Loton Park, which is right on the Welsh

Border. Deciding that it was time to visit his principality he walked to the first oak tree over the border and came back with a twig from it.

Loton is one of three manors given to John Leighton by Henry VII in return for loyal support in the events leading up to the Battle of Bosworth in 1485. In recent years the park has had a quite different reputation as a venue for motor sport. The village of Alberbury is tacked on to one side of it. The church has a fine series of memorials to the Leighton family and some fourteenth-century glass, and is altogether a noble building for a small village.

A right fork just outside Alberbury brings you to the A458 at Rowton Castle, a nineteenth-century structure which was once a school and is now being converted into flats.

We now go on to explore the Shropshire hills that lie to the south of Shrewsbury. There are three main groups, each with a distinctive character, and Shrewsbury is the starting point for the area to the south-west.

The road this time is the A488 for Bishop's Castle, which first of all passes through the dull dormitory village of Great Hanwood. (Connoisseurs of curious churches may find the time to turn right just after the village and travel the mile or so to Cruckton. The tiny church here is in a state of limbo — still open but no longer used for services, and it has a strange atmosphere, with its pews painted bright green, its tiny organ, single stained glass window and modern carved altar-cross.)

The double-peaked hill prominent to the left of the road is Pontesford Hill, and Pontesbury Hill lies just beyond it. The villages after which they are named also lie close together. By turning left at the Shell garage in Pontesford you can reach Shropshire's first nature reserve,

2
*

at Earl's Hill. It is best to leave the car in the village because the early part of the walk is of interest in itself, passing several relics of the lead-smelting industry that once flourished here. It is all fully described in the Shropshire Conservation Trust's booklet ' The Earl's Hill Nature Trail'.

More characteristic of the hills is Habberley, a hamlet reached by a turning from Pontesbury. It is a tiny place with a plain workaday church, and farms mingling with the old houses. The reason for the concentration of farms in the village is the fact that most of the land around here was common. The timber-framed Hall in Habberley was the home of a noted eighteenth-century historian William Mytton, a relative of 'Mad Jack' Mytton of Whittington, near Oswestry. It is best to return from Habberley by the Minsterley road which offers panoramic views across the Rea Valley.

Minsterley is much less pretentious than Pontesbury but has rather more of interest to the visitor. The church, one of the few in the county built in the seventeenth century, is of very distinctive design in red brick with prominent buttresses. The west end features a good deal of interesting carving, but the church is most famous for the 'maiden garlands' hanging high up at the back. Made of cloth and paper flowers, they were carried in the funeral processions of unmarried girls and then hung as a memorial in the church.

Minsterley Hall, a fine black and white manor house, lies behind the church, but the turnpike toll-booth, a few yards from the lych-gate, is rather more eye-catching, with its fanciful windows. It is in a poor state, but has recently acquired a preservation order.

You move into the hills by continuing along the A468 and turning left after a mile along a road signposted 'Snailbeach'. In front is a hillside covered with bracken and trees, and it is not until you reach the outskirts of Snailbeach that you notice the huge mounds of white waste and the derelict buildings and machinery of the former lead mines. Some idea of the extent of the workings here can be obtained by taking the left turn marked 'Lordshill' just beyond the spoil tips and walking the few yards to the plateau above, where machinery, sheds, chimneys and tramways are rapidly being reclaimed by nature.

Lead was mined in this area from Roman times, reaching a peak in the mid-nineteenth century. Interesting though it is to the industrial archaeologist, the area has a defeated air. When the mines were run down, more than an industry was lost. The miners occupied over a hundred smallholdings around here; very few survive, and ground that was previously cultivated is now disappearing beneath the bracken.

Various walks are possible on the ridge by continuing up the Lordshill road (definitely not for cars) and following the track to the summit. By walking south you can reach the most famous feature of this range — the Stiperstones. They are a series of jagged, quartzite outcrops with their highest point (1700ft) at the cluster of rocks called the 'Devil's Chair'. The forbidding atmosphere of the Stiperstones has given rise to a good deal of rather dark folklore, and there could hardly be a greater contrast with the pastoral valleys beneath.

An alternative way to the Devil's Chair is to pass through Snailbeach (ignoring the hamlet called The Stiperstones) and follow the road round to Bridges. At the Horseshoe Inn, cross

The unique west front of Minsterley Church

the road bridge over the East Onny river and take the steep, unfenced road. There is a left turn at Stedment Farm and you then pass Squilver Farm, which is now a holiday activity centre. The path to the ridge is then obvious.

The return to Shrewsbury can be made by going back from Bridges the way you came but turning left halfway to Snailbeach. This road goes through Shelve, another former mining village with industrial remains, and joins the A488 to the south of Hope. The journey along the main road then includes the attractive Hope Valley.

To the east of the Stiperstones is the famous Long Mynd. There is a 'back-door' route to it from Bridges, but the most interesting and dramatic approach is again from Shrewbury along the A49. As you leave the town, you pass near the suburb of Meole Brace, and for anyone interested in stained glass the church there, with its pre-Raphaelite windows designed by William Morris, is a compulsory stop. After leaving

Shrewsbury, the road is featureless for a mile or two, and it is worth a quick diversion along one of several roads to the left signposted 'Condover'.

Condover boasts one of the finest Elizabethan mansions in the country. Now a school for blind children, it is sometimes open during the summer holidays. The hall belonged to the Owen family, and their memorials are a feature of the church, which is also noted for its superb seventeenth-century oak roof and one of the first sculptures by the Victorian artist G F Watts.

Returning to the main road, you begin to see the sharp silhouette of a range of hills on the left and a vague, formless mass on the right. The former is the Caer Caradoc range, starting with the whale-backed Lawley but dominated by the pointed summit of Caer Caradoc itself. They loom over the road as you approach Church Stretton, and by comparison the Long Mynd to the right looks unspectacular. It has something of a Swiss air, with expensive-looking white houses peering out from the wooded hillside.

Church Stretton, the 'capital' of the Long Mynd, lies off the main road to the right. To reach it you cross a railway line and turn left very soon after for the car park (don't miss it — it is hard to find another one). Although the hills attract thousands of visitors each year, Church Stretton makes few concessions to tourism, apart from its excellent information centre tucked away behind the church at the top of the town. Here a wealth of information is available, and a visit immediately on arrival is advisable.

The town itself is a clean, tidy and well-bred place with the atmosphere of a superior spa, and indeed many attempts were made towards the end of the nineteenth century to turn it into one. The fact that it had no natural springs of its own did not deter the energetic Victorians; a 'hydropathic establishment' was built (now the Long Mynd Hotel) and plans were made to pipe water over from neighbouring Wentnor. The scheme was abandoned, but for a time water from Llandrindod Wells was transported here by train. Another enterprise, now obliterated by modern housing, was Samuel Bakewell's Private Lunatic Asylum for Gentlemen.

A walk round the town will reveal nothing very spectacular in the way of architecture, although there are some pleasant surprises, particularly in the Square, which has a good timber-framed building, formerly an inn, and an ironmonger's shop which is an outstanding example of Victorian shop design. St Laurence's church should not be missed. Before you enter the porch, walk round the left hand side and look at the Norman door with the 'Sheila na Gig' (a fertility figure) over it. The interior is noted for its magnificent roofs, embellished at the transept by a modern representation of St Laurence's symbol, a gridiron, with copper flames — a fine work, but not perhaps the most tactful memorial for the children who died in a hotel fire in the town.

The hills around Church Stretton are famous for containing some of the most ancient rocks known to geologists. The Long Mynd is composed of a wide variety of pre-Cambrian material at least seven million years old, which can be easily studied at natural outcrops or in the old quarries. The strata tend to be almost vertical. The distinctive characteristic of the Long Mynd is the series of 'batches', the local name for the deep ravines cutting into the hill from its south-eastern edge.

For those with limited time who want to sample the Long Mynd by car, the best starting point is Leebotwood, four miles north of Church Stretton on the A49. From here proceed to Woolstaston, which has a large earthwork and an attractive group of buildings round a village green (fairly rare in the border country). The church has many features of interest, especially the carving on the pulpit, lectern and altar-rails, done by a local man, William Hill. His fee came from the sales of a book by a nineteenth-century rector, Edmund Carr, who was caught in the snow while walking back from taking a service at Ratlinghope (pronounced 'Ratchup', incidentally). He survived for 27 hours, and his account of his ordeal had a great popular success.

Following the Ratlinghope road, you emerge eventually on to a heather-covered expanse of moorland, from which you descend again into a remote valley that is often inaccessible in winter. Just before Ratlinghope you turn left up a steep hill signposted 'Church Stretton', and this brings you to some of the most dramatic Long Mynd scenery, with magnificent views over innumerable neighbouring hills. You plunge back into Church Stretton by way of a road not recommended for drivers liable to vertigo.

There are many opportunities during this drive to stop and walk, but one or two routes for the more serious walker are recommended now.

The first starts by taking Burway Road out of Church Stretton. At the edge of the town there is a cattle grid

8
**

(GR 448942) at which you turn left. The Old Rectory Wood Nature Trail is on the left of this track, and is worth a diversion if you have time. Continue to the old reservoir, turn right and start climbing by the north side of the stream. At the head of the valley turn north to meet the metalled road, and follow it north-west until it forks. Take the right fork and then a track leading off to the right after a few hundred yards. The track branches after half a mile, and at the same point a path leads away to the right and takes you down into the Carding Mill Valley, a famous local beauty spot. The bottom of the valley is on the northern edge of the town.

The Carding Mill, incidentally, has now been converted for residential use, but it was once a flourishing weaving mill. A corn mill stood on the site as early as the fifteenth century.

At the sourthern end of the Long Mynd range, Minton is a good starting point for various walks. The lane in the centre of the village marked 'No Through Road' leads north-west under Packetstone Hill, and the subsequent path eventually meets the ancient Port Way. An alternative is to take the Hamperley road and branch off to the right after less than half a mile on to a path which takes you up Minton Batch. Both routes take you close to the Midland Gliding Club headquarters on the Port Way. By walking north on the Port Way you reach a path into Ashes Hollow and arrive back in Little Stretton.

The broad, smooth expanses of the Long Mynd are not to everyone's taste, and some visitors will be attracted by the sharp ridges of the Caer Caradoc range on the other side of the valley. The best approach is from the crossroads with traffic lights on the A49. Take the Hope Bowdler road and turn left almost immediately on to the old Roman road Watling Street. The lane off to the right which leads between Caer Caradoc and Helmeth Hill is clearly marked on the map. After a mile and a half a path to the summit of Caer Caradoc branches left.

The camp at the top is quite elaborate and is the subject of a detailed pamphlet available at the Information Centre — one of a series of leaflets about the local hills that are excellent value for money. As the name of the hill implies, it is one of several places claiming to be the site of the last stand of the British king Caradoc (Caratacus) in his campaign against the Romans. This final battle took place in about AD 50.

At the northern end of the range, the Lawley is less dramatic, but there is a good circular walk around it. It starts near Comley at GR 485968, passes along the bottom of the Lawley and meets a quiet road at the northern end. This lane takes you up on to Hoar Edge, where you branch off at GR 506976. From here tracks and lanes lead back to Church Stretton.

These walks are only a selection from dozens possible in the Church Stretton area; the dedicated rambler could spend a rewarding month or more around here. For the moment, however, it is time to look at the distinctive region known as the Clun Forest. The term 'forest' here and in the names 'Kerry Forest' and 'Radnor Forest' is used in its original sense of a large open space reserved for hunting. Paradoxically, trees would have been a nuisance then, but the Forestry Commission has been active in these areas in more recent times.

The Clun Forest is well-defined and symmetrical on the map, separated from the Long Mynd range by the river Camlad, enclosed to the west by a

curious bulge in the Welsh border
(crazily drawn in these parts), and to the
east by the Craven Arms-Knighton
road. Right in the centre, at the junction
of the four roads that divide the Forest
into quarters, is Clun itself.

The route from Church Stretton is the
A49 to Craven Arms and then the
B4368. Craven Arms is an odd place.
From the main road it seems to consist
of a string of miscellaneous functional
buildings, and, although there is a
residential area away from the road, it
did start life as a purely functional town.
Situated at the junction of two lines, it
was a convenient railway depot for the
embarking and disembarking of
enormous numbers of sheep which were
herded here for the periodic sales and
then carried to all parts of the country. It
still has the sales, but the sheep now
travel by road. Its most distinguished
building is the early nineteenth-century
hotel from which it took its name.

Turning right at the hotel, for Clun on
the B4368; it is worth turning off at
Aston on Clun to visit Hopesay, snugly
situated among the hills. The church is

of some interest, with a fine medieval
roof and a wealth of carving. Hopesay
Common, to the east, is National Trust
property and makes a pleasant short
walk; it is reached by a lane to the right,
a few hundred yards beyond the church.
When you re-join the main road at
Aston, note the stunted tree decked with
flags. They commemorate the marriage
of a local lady in the eighteenth century,
although earnest scholars theorise about
early pagan cults.

This south-east quarter of the Forest
is best known because of the jingle:

'Clunton, Clunbury, Clungunford and
Clun

Are the quietest places under the sun.'
Perhaps this is the place to point out
that, contrary to what every book on the
area says, A. E. Housman did not write
these lines, although he used them to
preface one of his poems in *A Shropshire
Lad*. What he did say was that this
district is:

'A country for easy livers
The quietest under the sun.'
Unfortunately there is not much at
Clunton, Clunbury or Clungunford to
delay the visitor, but Clun is another
matter.

Its layout is typical of many small
border towns that started promisingly
but never developed. The original
settlement is around the church on the
south bank of the river, while across the
bridge is the grid-patterned borough
that grew up around the castle.

The dominant feature of the church is
the massive Norman tower, with a
pyramid roof added in the seventeenth
century, and the interior is unexpectedly
rich and spacious, displaying some fine
woodwork and handsome arcades. As
you go out through the eighteenth-
century lychgate, the town lies beneath
you, with the gaunt castle away to the
left. You get to it by crossing the

**PLACES OF INTEREST IN THE CLUN
FOREST**

Clun Castle
Substantial three-storey keep,
massive earthworks.

Holy Trinity Hospital, Clun
Seventeenth-century almshouses with
chapel.

Heath House, Leintwardine
Early seventeenth-century house,
celebrated staircase of c1700. Open
by appointment (see Further
Information).

The massive tower of Clun church

picturesque bridge with its recesses for pedestrians. The castle is impressive not so much for its surviving ruins — mainly a three-storey keep — as for the huge earthworks around it. The town's other main attraction is the Holy Trinity Hospital, a charming group of seventeenth-century almshouses with a chapel.

3
*
A road leads past the almshouses to a youth hostel, and this is the start of a walk to the big hill fort of Bury Ditches. Go a mile or so to Guilden Down and take the track marked on the map at GR 310827. Unlike most of these forts it is now buried in a plantation and can take some finding, but the walk is pleasant enough, even if you fail.

Four miles to the south-east of Clun is Hopton Castle, a village with a fine old black and white house that was once the rectory. The castle from which it gets its name was the scene of a bloody incident during the Civil War, when a group of Parliamentary soldiers was massacred by Royalists after a siege lasting three weeks.

In the middle of the north-eastern quarter of the Forest is Lydbury North, the important centre of a very extensive manor in Saxon times. King Offa gave it to the Bishop of Hereford and his successors in the eighth century, and the new castle which the Bishop built a few miles to the west became known as Bishop's Castle.

Bishop's Castle is now a sleepy town with little sense of its former importance, which can be gauged by the fact that until 1832 it returned two MPs to Parliament, and that it survived until 1967 as Britain's smallest municipal borough. The tiny Town Hall still stands at the top of the High Street, complete with cells beneath, and next to it is the quaint 'house on crutches' — a Tudor building with one end supported on wooden posts.

Behind the Town Hall is the Castle Hotel, which has the remains of the castle in its grounds. The main street runs long and straight from here down to the church, which was largely rebuilt after suffering extensive damage during the Civil War. Other notable buildings here are Old Hall, a fine Tudor house to the east of the church, and the 'Three Tuns', a seventeenth-century inn with its own brewhouse next door.

The western half of the Clun Forest merges into the moorland 'desert' that stretches from Newtown in the north to Builth Wells in the south, including most of the old county of Radnorshire. It is an area of undulating hills, partly afforested, at an average height of 1500ft.

Mainstone, four miles west of Bishop's Castle, is one of the few settlements in this part of the Forest. Its church is a mile away at Churchtown and has in it a two-hundredweight boulder, once used as a test of strength by young men of the parish. Almost due south is Newcastle, a rather larger place, also with a detached church and several earthworks round it. Both villages are next to Offa's Dyke, which survives for long stretches in this area; the long-distance footpath follows it closely, and forms a central 'spine' from which other walks radiate.

The OS map shows many possibilities for the long-distance walker, who has the chance to see here some of the finest surviving stretches of Offa's Dyke. The following suggestions are for walks of moderate length.

Take the waymarked Dyke path north from Churchtown (GR 263873), just to the west of the church, and turn left on to the second lane crossing the path. This takes you across Edenhope Hill and down to Two Crosses. Go straight over at the crossroads here, along the Ridgeway known as Skelton's Bank, and re-join the Dyke path at Hergan in order to return to Churchtown. (A shorter walk is possible by turning left at Two Crosses.)   **6 ****

Three other walks in the south of the Forest have a convenient main road starting point at Five Turnings (GR 286755). To the west is a circular walk around Cwmsanaham Hill, crossing the Dyke twice.   **4½ ****   To the east is a lane which leads across Stow Hill, down to the river Redlake and across to Bedston Hill and the ancient Castle Ditches; this is a forested area with many tracks. North-east from Five Turnings a lane runs to   **6 . ****   Wax Hall. Very shortly after this, a track to the right will take you to the summit of Caer Caradoc.   **4 ****

The area to the north and west of the Clun Forest, of a very similar character, is described in later chapters.

4 Welshpool, Montgomery and Newtown

Chapter 1 ended at the border village of Llanymynech, on the main road from Oswestry to Welshpool, and for many visitors, the journey into Wales will begin on this road. As if to signal the border and Breidden group of hills rears up dramatically out of the plain the dominate the scene as you drive south. Like many similar isolated hills they were produced by volcanic action, and

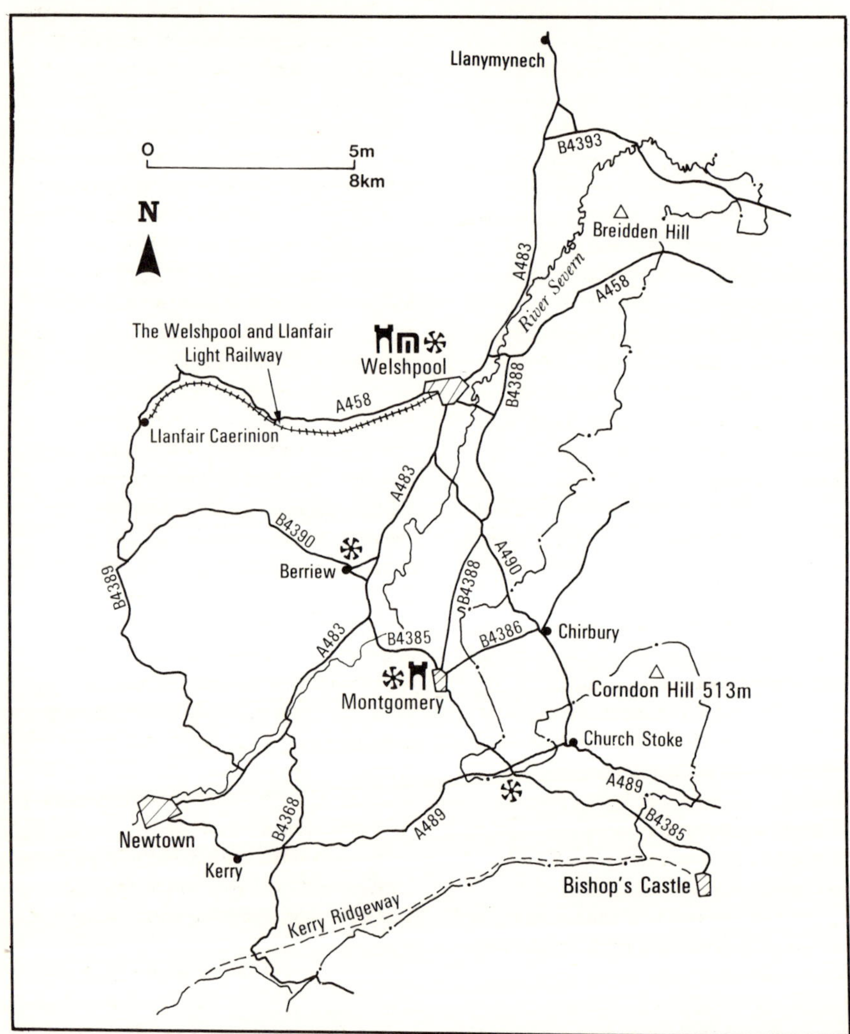

the quality of their stone has made them the target of elaborate quarrying.

There are three peaks, the nearest being the Breidden itself, surmounted by a column in memory of Admiral Rodney — he was not a local man, but the needs of the navy in which he served meant a profitable local trade in timber. The other two summits are Moel-y-Golfa and Middletown Hill, and the whole group provides a bracing walk that starts at Criggion. You can reach the village by turning on to the B4393 at Four Crosses and then turning right shortly after Llandrinio, undeterred by the sinister radio masts.

Criggion is a sketchy place. As you come into it and see the Breidden at close quarters, you realise that the trees that cover it are hiding precipitous, scree-covered slopes, the result of years of quarrying. The prim-looking red-brick church is on the left, and the route to the top starts a little way after the telephone box on the right. It leads first to Middletown Hill, and there are various tracks on the top connecting the three summits.

Having re-joined the A483 after the diversion to the hills you travel between the Montgomery Canal and the river Severn, with the Long Mountain looming on the left. About a mile past Pool Quay the canal is virtually beside the road, and over to the left is the site of Strata Marcella, a huge twelfth-century abbey, now just an earthwork called Abbey Bank.

The abbey survived four hundred years of upheaval and strife, only to be destroyed by an act of sixteenth-century vandalism. Court records show that an enterprising man called Nicholas Purcell acquired the lease after the dissolution of the abbey by Henry VIII and proceeded to sell it piecemeal throughout a wide area. The bells went to Chirk, the organ to Shrewsbury, and valuable building materials went in all directions, including Oswestry castle for repair work. But for Purcell the ruins would have been some of the most important and extensive in the country.

Just before Welshpool the Shrewsbury road turns off to the left, and on the canal immediately above this point is Buttington wharf, the starting-point for special narrow-boat trips for disabled people. The Prince of Wales did much to encourage this project, which was accompanied by the restoration of a long stretch of canal north of Welshpool. The Shrewsbury road here leads to Buttington itself, its neat church a rare example of the eighteenth-century restoration of a medieval building. The river crossing was once of vital importance and great strategic value. It is mentioned in Welsh legends and has been the focus of many tracks and roads as well as border battles.

The large estate to the south of Buttington is Leighton Park, a fascinating subject of more recent history. A Liverpool banker, John Naylor, had the Hall built and the grounds laid out in 1851. The work included a parish church with a family mausoleum. Naylor tried various enterprises including the planting of many trees, among them a grove of Redwoods now in the care of the Royal Forestry Society. He was a pioneer in progressive agriculture. His farm buildings were brand new, and, like the Hall and church, lit by gas from his own gasworks. Elaborate waterworks drove turbines to power machinery. Most remarkable, perhaps, was a tank of liquid fertiliser on a hill with a system of pipes to the fields; a funicular railway carried the contents of the fertiliser to the tank.

Very little now survives. The estate

Welshpool High Street

was broken up after the First World War, and the house has since had a succession of owners. The Offa's Dyke path runs through the park, and you can join it at GR 247034, where it begins to follow forestry tracks. When you reach Pant-y-bwch you can either follow the road down or extend the walk by continuing up the path to Beacon Ring, a famous hill fort. If you go on from there, you will emerge at School House in Buttington.

It is worth continuing along the B4388 and turning off for Welshpool at Lower Leighton. This road passes the fine railway station, unusually grand for a small town, but erected in the belief that Cambrian Railways were to make their headquarters there. That honour eventually went to Oswestry. After passing up Severn Street and reaching the traffic lights, turn right, and right again almost immediately, for the main car park.

Welshpool is one of those towns whose main attraction is a homely and undistinguished collection of domestic architecture. Its one attempt at grandeur — a florid, khaki Town Hall — sticks out like a sore thumb in the long and harmonious line of Mount Street, High Street, Broad Street and Severn Street, which form the main thoroughfare through the town.

At summer weekends, Welshpool is a kind of Clapham Junction for tourists entering or leaving mid-Wales; in the winter it settles to its traditional role of rural shopping centre and important cattle market. A walk round the town can conveniently start at the main car park near the church. Turn left, then right and you are in Broad Street, which lives up to its name, providing pleasantly spacious shopping accommodation. The shops here are mainly eighteenth and nineteenth century, with some modern fronts grafted on, but there are some well-restored half-timbered buildings, too.

The first turning on the left, New Street, contains a cockpit restored to its original condition and squeamishly under-publicised in the tourist literature. Almost opposite the Town Hall is a pedestrian way to Powis Castle, described later, and a little further on is a craft shop, worth investigating for its fifteenth-century architecture, as well as for its wares.

At the top of the hill the town appears to be petering out, but if you continue down the other side you will come to a roundabout and the Raven Square terminus of the Welshpool and Llanfair Light Railway. It has the usual slightly eccentric history of determined volunteer effort. Opened in 1903 with a 2′6″ gauge, it ran the nine miles from Llanfair Caereinion to Welshpool with passengers and goods. Surprisingly it survived until 1956, when falling demand and competition from road transport forced its closure. Almost at once a preservation society was formed, and seven years later the railway re-

PLACES OF INTEREST IN AND AROUND WELSHPOOL

Powis Castle, 1m south of town on A483
Continuously inhabited for 500 years. Fine furniture and decoration, collection of Indian art, terraced gardens, park.

Powysland Museum, Church Street
Local history and life, including Bronze Age and Roman exhibits. Also art gallery.

Cockpit
Restored eighteenth-century cockfighting pit in New Street. Ask for key at house next to The Vaults in New Street.

Trelydan Hall, 3m north of town
Restored Tudor House. Costume displays. Day and residential courses in floral art and certain crafts. Dinners with traditional entertainment.

Canal Cruises, Canal Wharf, Severn Street
1½ hour cruises in narrowboat, from July to September. Welshpool 3271 for details.

Montgomery Castle, 9m south of Welshpool
Ruins with panoramic views. Small museum of local life in town centre.

Armoury Recreation Centre, Welshpool, Brook Street
Badminton, squash, table-tennis etc. Refreshments.

Swimming pool, at bottom end of Severn Street.

Welshpool and Llanfair Light Railway, Welshpool terminus at Raven Square
2′6″ gauge restored line, variegated rolling stock and locomotives. Headquarters with displays, souvenirs etc. at Llanfair Caereinion, at other end of line.

Powis Castle, Welshpool

opened rather shakily with a distinct shortage of rolling stock.

With the luck that rewards the brave, the company was able to acquire cheaply an engine built by the French under German occupation, plus some brand-new coaches that happened to fit the gauge. For some time the engine ran in the incongruous livery of the Austrian Alpine Railway, and since then the company has made a speciality of collecting foreign rolling stock.

5
******
If you want to explore some interesting country to the west of Welshpool and perhaps watch the trains go by at the same time, you can take the path by the Raven pub close to the terminus. Make for Talyrnau and then go on to the hill fort at Pen-y-foel. Syfaen station is a short distance away, and you have the choice of taking a brief train-ride back or following the A458 a few yards east and taking the path up to Y Golfa. From the top a track leads back to Welshpool through Llanerchydol park.

From the Raven Square roundabout, the rather featureless Union Street brings you to the parish church of St Mary. Opposite the door is a stone said to be the throne of the Abbot of Strata Marcella. Round the corner in Church Street the Powysland Museum has displays of bygone local life.

The showpiece of Welshpool is undoubtedly Powis Castle, which can be reached on foot from Broad Street or by car along Red Lane, a turning off the Newtown road about a mile from the town centre. It once dominated the whole area, but now conceals itself behind magnificent trees; its vast red bulk comes as a surprise. Like all border castles it has seen plenty of action, but thanks to substantial Elizabethan restoration and the reluctance of the Parliamentarians to destroy it during the Civil War, it has remained inhabited for five hundred years. As with Chirk Castle its uncompromising exterior is a strange contrast to the comfort and splendour within.

Outstanding features are a massive seventeenth-century staircase, a Long Gallery with Elizabethan plaster-work, and a collection of Indian art started by Robert Clive and continued by his son, the first modern Earl of Powis. There is also a state bedroom designed for Charles I. The superb gardens were laid out by Capability Brown, and the park (open for most of the year without charge) is notable for its trees, including a Douglas Fir said to be the tallest tree in Britain. Although the castle was given to the National Trust in 1952 the present Earl still lives there.

Powis Castle has been only discreetly commercialised; a rather more thorough job has been done at Trelydan Hall, which can be reached by taking the A490 out of Welshpool and turning right after about a mile. But even those who are put off by 'romantic honeymoon rooms', 'a private self-catering Georgian unit' or 'candle-lit dinners with Welsh harpists and clog dancers' can still admire the restoration work on this magnificent Tudor house.

5½
**

Trelydan can be included in a walk to the north of Welshpool. Take the minor road by the Powysland Museum until you reach the A490. Turn right to Coed-y-wlad, where a track and path lead north to Guilsfield. The parish church is well worth a visit. Follow the minor road east out of Guilsfield, turning off on to a path after half a mile. Tracks and lanes then take you past Trelydan and back to the town.

1
*

Should you decide to take the train to Llanfair Caereinion other walks are possible. There is a gentle stroll through the Deri Wood (now a park and picnic area), across the footbridge and back to the town on the other side of the river.

4½
**

For a rather longer walk go up Watergate Street, turn right at the crossroads, turn left at the telephone box after a mile and a half, and then left at the next crossroads. This brings you back to the town by way of Gibbet Hill, with fine views of the Banwy Valley.

5
**

A third suggestion is to take the B4385 out of the town and after a quarter of a mile turn left on to the track at GR 108064. Follow the track and path east to GR 132069, then follow the lane round north and west, returning to the starting point by way of the path beginning at GR 123075. (This walk, though not particularly high, goes through very deserted country.)

Newtown can be reached from Welshpool either by the fast main road or by less-frequented minor routes. The short run on the A483 is exhilarating, passing through the broad Severn valley and some characteristic border countryside — lush pasture, wooded hills, black and white cottages and the occasional red-brick mansion set well up on the higher ground to avoid flooding. The canal, clean and bright after recent clearing, follows the road for much of the way.

The only village of any size on the route is Berriew, worth a visit for its attractive, half-timbered buildings and some interesting canal features. One of

Decorated houses at Kerry

these is a small aqueduct, built in 1796 and restored a hundred years later (GR 188006); another is Rectory Lock and its cottage, reached by walking north along the towpath from the canal bridge just before the village. Browsing canal enthusiasts will find a good deal more, including some old wharfing. Opposite the point where the road to Berriew branches from the A483 is an ancient track leading down to the Severn. At one side of it is a monolith called Maen Bueno, traditionally of Bronze Age origin and used as a pulpit by St Bueno.

Anyone interested in railway history should stop off at Abermule, between Berriew and Newtown. A road turns off here for Kerry twisting and turning up a steep hill. Incredibly this was also the route for a railway line, designed optimistically to serve the sheep farms of

the Kerry area. It was never profitable and did not survive long, but parts of the trackbed are still visible to the left of the Kerry road.

The other route to Newtown is leisurely and very rewarding. About a mile and a half south of Welshpool the A490 branches left from the main Newtown road and soon begins to climb steeply, giving extensive views over the Severn valley. Follow the signs for Montgomery and soon a long, straight switchback of a road brings you into the miniature town that was once the 'capital' of the county that used to bear its name. Little more than a village in size, it had borough status and still boasts a Town Hall, standing at the head of a mellow main street that is more like a square.

The ruined thirteenth-century castle

Old Oswestry, Iron Age fort

Coleham Pumping Engine, Shrewsbury

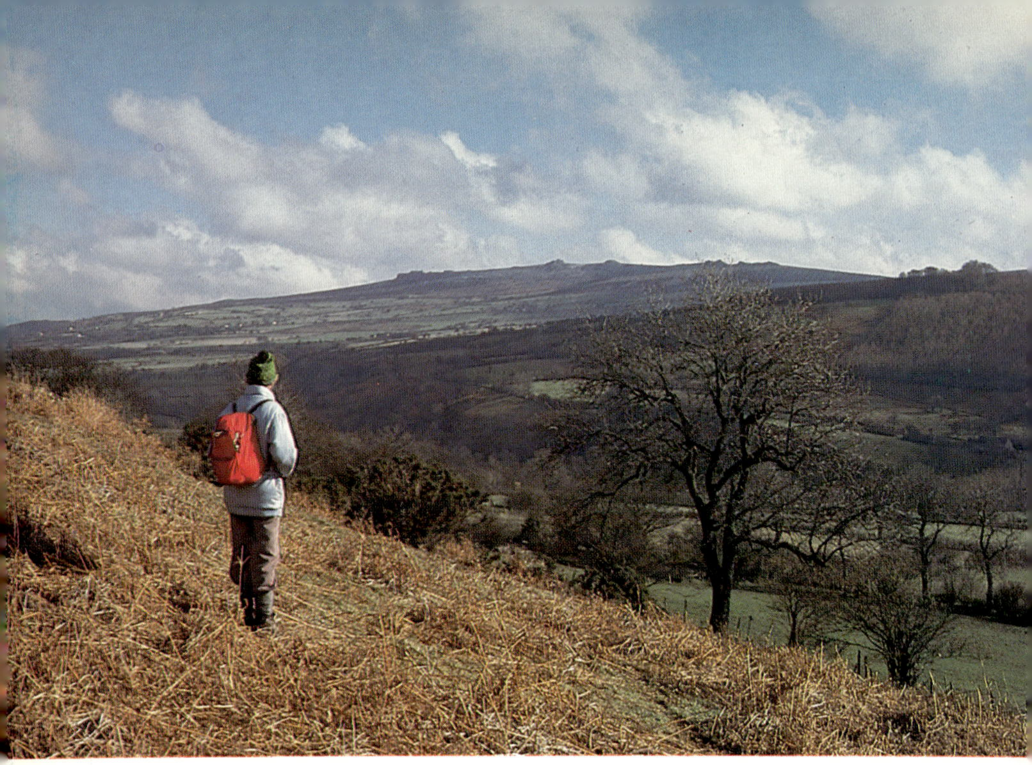

Mucklewich Hill to the Stiperstones

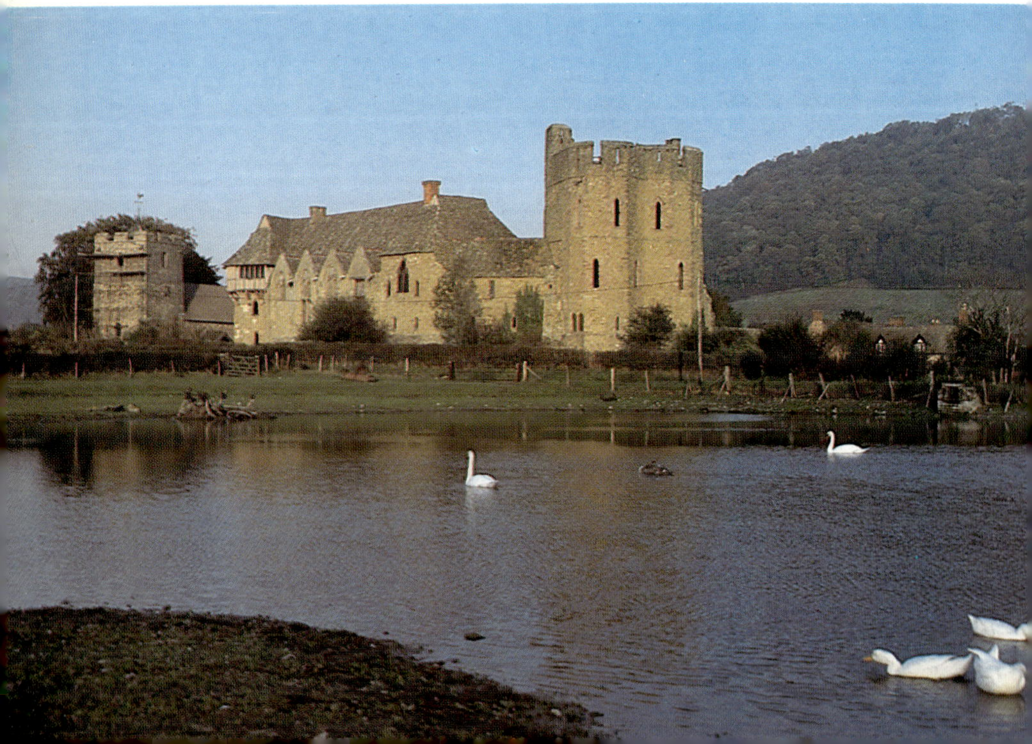

*The Old Parish Church and Robert
Owen's tomb, Newtown*

towers above the town, and apart from
its historical interest provides
spectacular views which must have been
an asset to defenders guarding what has
been a strategic route for thousands of
years. The path to the castle starts
behind the Town Hall.

Montgomery has its curiosities, too.
Immediately below the castle are the
easily-identifiable remains of the old
county gaol, now private property, while
in the churchyard is the celebrated
'Robber's Grave'. John Davies was
hanged in 1821 for highway robbery. He
maintained that the evidence against
him was false, and no grass could ever
grow on his grave.

A recent innovation in the centre of
the town is the Old Bell, a folk museum
concerned with local life and history,
providing permanent displays and
special exhibitions.

The Montgomery Civic Society
publishes a leaflet called 'A Walk
Around Montgomery', which gives more
detailed information about the town and
is well worth the small charge. A more
ambitious walk starts at the entrance to
the castle grounds by way of a lane
leading to the Town Hill Monument
(exceptional views from here). Continue
south to the junction at GR 218945, turn
east, then south again very shortly after.
Make for the junction with the A489 at
GR 225927 (route clear on map). After
half a mile on the main road turn right
on to the path which leads into
Bacheldre.

6
**

Textile Museum, Commercial Street
Machinery and other exhibits relating
to former woollen industry, housed
in former weaving shops.

Davies Memorial Gallery, Newtown
Hall Park
Gallery founded in memory of the
Misses Davies of Gregynog. Touring
exhibitions only.

Old Parish Church, off Broad Street
Tower and other remains. Tomb of
Robert Owen.

Dolerw Park
30-acre riverside park. Access from
Newtown Hall Park by suspension
bridge.

Alaven Designs, Cymric Mill, Canal
Road
Workshop producing leather goods.
Other craft products for sale. Visitors
welcome.

W.H. Smith's Shop, Town Centre
This shop has been restored to its
original 1920s style and layout.

Street Market
In town centre on Tuesdays.

Gregynog Hall, 5m north-west of
Newtown
Gardens and park normally open to
public.

Theatr Hafren, Llanidloes Road
In Montgomery College of Further
Education. All forms of
entertainment.

Royal Welsh Warehouse
Home of world's first mail-order
business. Near Newtown station.

Bacheldre Water Mill, near
Churchstoke, 15m east of Newtown
on A489
Water-powered flour mill in
operation.

Bacheldre is of some interest because
it contains one of the few water-powered
flour mills still working. You will find it
just off the main road at GR 243928 and
visitors are welcome. The mill is about
two hundred years old, and although
commercial working stopped in the 60s
it is still functional and is being restored
to full use.

4½
**

You can complete a circular walk by
way of the Offa's Dyke path to the
north, which crosses the A489 at GR
250933. After two miles, turn left on to
the track which passes through Lymore
and brings you back to Montgomery.

The poet George Herbert lived in

Montgomery Castle, and there are
further associations with the Herbert
family at Chirbury, about three miles
north-east on the B4386. Lord Herbert
of Chirbury, the poet's elder brother, left
the village a large number of chained
books, which were housed in the
vicarage until taken over by the County
Archivist at Shrewsbury. It is an
unspoilt village, with a
disproportionately large church, the
nave of which was formerly part of a
thirteenth-century priory. In the shadow
of the church is the black and white
seventeenth-century school.

The route is now the A490 to

Churchstoke, a village of a kind which will now be familiar — homely, random in pattern, with a pleasant mixture of brick and half-timber and generally reflecting the practicalities of country living.

There is a good opportunity here to climb Corndon Hill which is so prominent to the east. About a quarter of a mile from the village centre on the A489 (east) take the lane leading off to the left. The first lane on the right brings you to Old Churchstoke. From here a lane and path, clear on the map, take you to the top.

You take the Newtown road out of Churchstoke and soon pass the turning for Bacheldre, mentioned earlier as the home of an eighteenth-century watermill. The road lies beneath hills which will be explored later, and the last stop before Newtown is at Kerry. Here there is a chance to study at close quarters a peculiar characteristic of this part of the border — ordinary brick cottages painted with black stripes to give the impression of half-timbering.

Half a mile east of Kerry, at Glan Mule, was the terminus of the ill-fated Kerry Railway, referred to earlier. Any enthusiast wishing to trace its course should start at GR 165904.   After

The millpond at Bacheldre, near Church Stoke

Kerry, the road drops very steeply down into Newtown. If Welshpool now moves at the leisurely pace of an agricultural centre, Newtown still retains a more urgent commercial bustle, especially on Tuesdays when the market stalls spread on to the main streets. It is literally a new town, having been designated as the main development area of mid-Wales. New housing has spread rapidly and the population has risen sharply in recent years.

None of this has affected the old town centre. Newtown has a fascinating history as a centre of the textile industry, and, in particular, the production of the famous Welsh flannel, worn by the Duke of Wellington's army and (thanks to mail order) by slaves in America. In the nineteenth century, Newtown and nearby Llanidloes had large factories producing woollen cloth; at the peak of production it is estimated that the town contained 35 spinning mills and 82 weaving establishments. It could easily rival the Yorkshire textile towns, and was in fact known as 'The Leeds of Wales'.

The big mills have now gone, but some significant reminders are still to be seen. Cross the main river bridge at the end of Broad Street, turn right into Commercial Street, and within a hundred yards on the left is the Textile Museum. It is a small building, but the plaque at the door reveals that it was built to house six families on the ground floor and over twenty handlooms on the first floor. It requires little imagination to visualise the conditions in which the weavers lived and worked.

The last building before the bridge on the return route is one of the original mills, converted in 1947 into a Roman Catholic church. In stark contrast to these small work-places is the Royal Welsh Warehouse, which can hardly be missed at the other end of the town near the station. Pryce Jones started the world's first mail-order business here in 1859, specialising in flannel, and his warehouse is a huge monument to the industry.

Newtown's most famous son was Robert Owen, philanthropist and pioneer of the Co-operative Movement. He was born here in 1771 and left at the age of ten. Thirteen years later he was manager of the vast New Lanark mills in Scotland, where he started an unprecedented welfare programme for his workers, including superior housing and working conditions and medical care. He proved to sceptical colleagues that contented factory workers were the key to profitable production.

Owen was buried in Newtown in 1858. His tomb can be seen beside the remains of the old Parish Church off Broad Street. The ruins are interesting in themselves since they include the substantial tower and timber belfry, and the whole area is an island of peace with its well-maintained gardens. The new church is an impressive brick building at the southern end of the town; if you go to look at it, note also the magnificent Baptist Church opposite, reflecting more clearly than anything else Newtown's former wealth.

Newtown's new status has brought some fine amenities, among them the large Dolerw Park by the river and the splendid Theatr Hafren, housed in the Montgomeryshire College of Further Education out on the Llanidloes road.

The Davies Memorial Gallery is a reminder of another local boy who made good. David Davies started work as a sawyer in Llandinam, about seven miles west of the town, and ended his life as Lord Davies of Llandinam. He was behind much of the mining development in South Wales, establishing Barry

Docks as a port for coal exports. He also helped to finance several railway projects in mid-Wales. His home in later life was Gregynog Hall near the village of Tregynon, and after his death his daughters offered the Hall as a centre for the encouragement of Welsh culture. Today the Hall is an outpost of the University of Wales, but part of the large park is open and a nature trail has been established in it.

4 ★ A circular walk through parkland at Gregynog is possible by taking the Skew Bridge road out of Tregynon, branching off at GR 088981 and walking south-west to Bwlch-y-ffridd. The return track is to the south of, and roughly parallel to, the first track.

On the other side of Newtown the Kerry Forest provides some fine walking country. Much of it is planted with Forestry Commission conifers, but generally the area is high, open and windswept. For those who want a long-distance walk there is the Kerry Ridgeway, fifteen miles of ancient drover's road of particular interest to the archaeologist. The Ridgeway can be used as the basis for a variety of shorter walks since there are innumerable paths leading down from it, most of them ending at the A489.

15 ★★

The starting point of the Ridgeway is reached by taking the tortuous A483 out of Newtown and turning left at Dolfor (signposted Knighton). This is the B4355, and the Ridgeway starts at Cider House Farm, about two miles along it.

The first feature of interest on the track is the Cross Dyke, an earth work created possibly in the sixth century BC as a local territorial boundary. Two similar sites occur about six miles further on; known as the Upper and Lower Short Ditch, they are encountered at each end of the stretch of track which passes through the Long Plantation. Very shortly after the Cross Dyke the track passes two Two Tumps, Bronze Age burial mounds, which have been excavated to reveal early stone tools.

Soon after the beginning of the Long Plantation a track off to the right leads to the Cantlin Stone. The popular story is that two neighbouring parishes argued over who was responsible for burying a man who died while walking on the Ridgeway. Eventually he was buried in Bettws-y-Crwyn churchyard, and the stone was erected where he died, to record the fact.

After another three miles the Ridgeway becomes a road at the hamlet of Pant Glas. Taking the right-hand fork here you arrive shortly at Offa's Dyke, which crosses the road at right angles. Incidentally you are literally walking on the Welsh border because this road forms the boundary between Powys and Shropshire. The Caer Din Ring, an Iron Age hill fort, can be seen on the left shortly after the crossroads at Hazel Bank, and about a mile further on is the fine motte and bailey at Bishopsmoat. It stands 1100ft above sea level and is Shropshire's highest castle. The road then descends into Bishop's Castle.

7 ★★ Those who want a shorter walk on these uplands can take the Kerry road out of Newtown and turn off on the B4368 a mile after Kerry. After two miles, this road goes through Block Wood and crosses the Ridgeway on the other side. If you start to walk west along the Ridgeway from this point, you come to the Two Tumps and Cross Dyke after two miles. At Two Tumps a path branches south around Cilfaesty Hill to Panty Hill and then leads down to Rhuddw Brook (GR 159837). Keeping left on this track brings you back to the starting-point.

5 Radnor

This chapter covers an area approximately that of the old county of Radnorshire, now part of Powys, but retaining its identity as the District of Radnor. It has the distinction of being one of the largest local government districts in England and Wales, but has a permanent population of not much more than 20,000.

A sixteenth-century writer said of it: 'The air thereof is sharp and cold for that the snow lieth and lasteth long unmelted under the shadowing high hills and overhanging rocks. The soil is hungry, rough and churlish and hardly bettered by painful labour'. Not surprisingly the economy of Radnor has been traditionally based on sheep, although in recent years forestry has become an important factor.

Fortunately very little has been done to change the characteristic appearance of this deserted area. It is a countryside of bare, undulating hills and moorland, with frequent higher and more massive ranges and sudden sharp ridges. As you move through it, the hills constantly assume new patterns in a confusing way. It is fine walking country, but to be treated with caution. Like much border hill country it appears perfectly safe until you take a wrong turning, when the absence of prominent landmarks or human habitation can be frightening.

Radnor is enclosed by rivers — the Teme to the north, the Lugg to the east, the Wye to the south and the Ithon to the west, while the Aran cuts across the middle. Exploring it is a matter of striking inwards from the valleys.

As you move south from Newtown on the A483 you are aware at once of being in a different kind of country. The road climbs steadily through a series of tortuous bends, and the Severn valley gradually disappears from view. After about six miles the road winds in spectacular fashion round Glog Hill, and shortly afterwards the river Ithon appears on the right. The first village of any size is Llanbadarn Fynydd. It is unremarkable in itself, but is the centre of a complex network of walks (clearly shown on the OS map) offering expeditions of any length and variety. From the point of view of clothing and protection, you need to bear in mind that you are at a thousand feet before you start climbing. Convenient access to the hills is by way of the lane leading north-east out of Llanbadarn.

Three miles south of it you pass on the left a picnic place and some thoughtfully-sited toilets. This is a good place to stop because a hundred yards further on, nestling under the road to the right, is the church of Llananno. In the subsequent chapters there will be many references to rood-screens, but Llananno is reckoned to have the finest in Wales. It is a miracle of fifteenth-century carving, and equally miraculous is the fact that it was carefully replaced when the church was restored in the nineteenth century. Its origin is uncertain — according to tradition it came from the abbey at Cwmhir, further south.

Very soon after Llananno comes the sizeable village of Llanbister, now by-passed by the main road, but worth turning off for, in order to see another

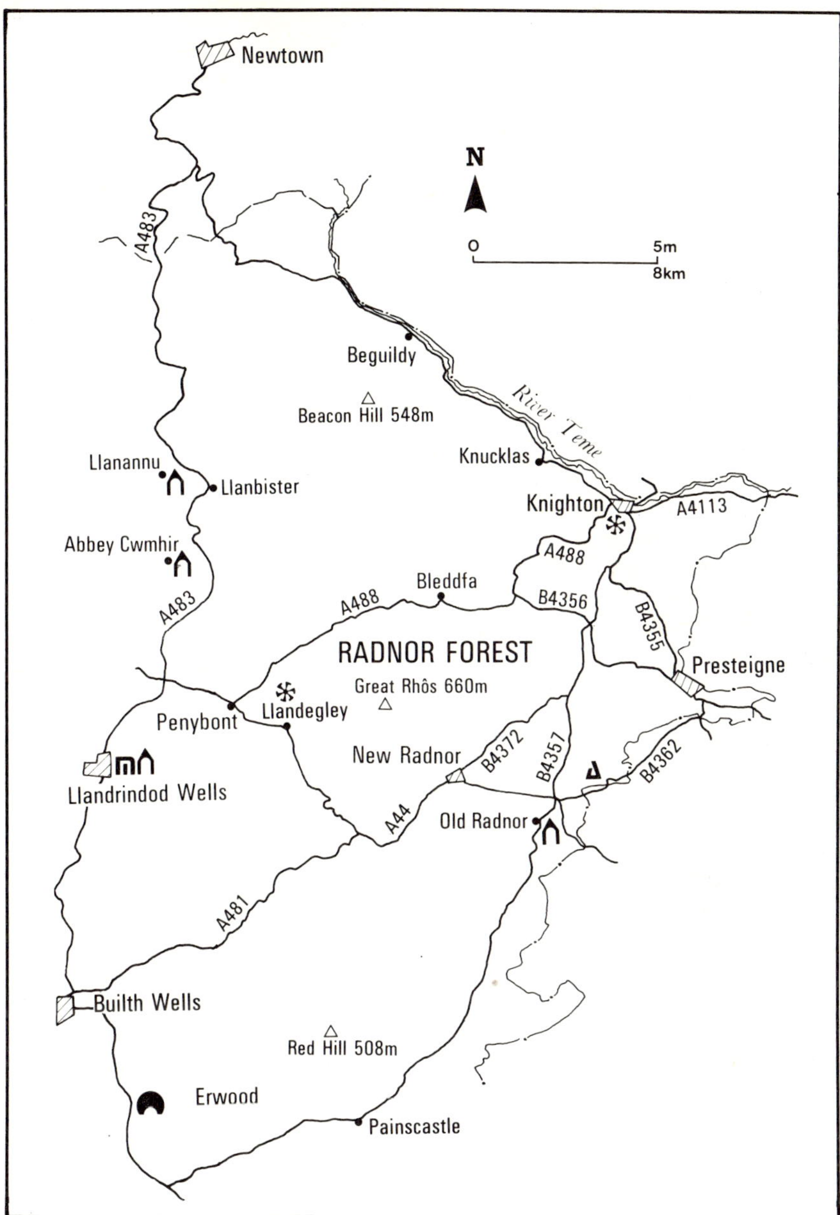

rare piece of church architecture — an eighteenth-century choir loft with a tiny schoolroom below. The main features of interest at Llandewi Ystradenny, four miles further on, are the twin hill forts to the north. They can be reached on foot by a track to the left of the main road about a quarter of a mile before the village centre. It is a steep but satisfying walk.

$2\frac{1}{2}$
**

4½
**

Half a mile beyond Llandewi the road crosses the Ithon, and the bridge is a good starting point for a walk to the ruins of the famous Abbey Cwmhir. The route starts as a lane, becomes a track and then joins a metalled road. Motorists will need to go another mile or so to the signposted turning, on to a road which can be congested in the holiday season.

The abbey was a twelfth-century Cistercian foundation in a typically remote spot. When building started the plan obviously allowed for enormous size — it would certainly have been the largest abbey in Wales and among the largest in Britain. The 242ft nave is exceeded only by those of York, Durham and Winchester cathedrals. It comes as a surprise, therefore, to find that this huge building was designed for about fifty monks. In fact it was never completed. The abbey's history was one of instability, as it found itself caught between the ambitions of the Welsh princes and the English kings. It suffered attacks from both sides, even when under the protection of the powerful Mortimer family; indeed it was finally destroyed by Owain Glyndwr in 1401 as part of his campaign against the Mortimers.

The abbey ruins featured in another episode of history. During the Civil War they were fortified by Royalist sympathisers, only to be captured by Sir Thomas Middleton. After this it had a succession of private owners, and archaeological investigations in the early nineteenth century uncovered a great many relics. Little remains today (the tradition that the grave of Llewelyn ap Gruffydd, last of the native Princes of Wales, is located here is open to doubt) but six of the original nave arches were built into Llanidloes church when it was enlarged, and can be seen there today.

PLACES OF INTEREST IN AND AROUND LLANDRINDOD WELLS

Museum, Memorial Gardens, Temple Street
Exhibits from Castell Collen Roman fort, town history, also doll collection.

Vintage bicycles, collection at Automobile Palace
Exhibits from era 1869 to 1938.

Albert Hall, Ithon Street
Centre for plays, concerts etc.

Rock Park and Pump Room
Dell with labyrinth of paths around a stream. Refreshments at the Pump Room.

Bowling greens
Venue for international as well as local competitions.

Lake and Common
Fishing, boating, putting, crazy golf etc. refreshments.

Abbey Cwmhir, 6m due north of Llandrindod, off A483
Important site of major medieval abbey.

Elan Valley, 15m west of Llandrindod, via A4081
Birmingham Corporation reservoir system, spectacular dams. Accessible by car.

Penybont Pottery, north-east of Llandrindod at junction of A44 and A488
Visitors welcome to watch work in progress.

Llandrindod Wells

Also traceable are the remains of the system of fishponds fed by the nearby river Clwedog.

After the diversion to Abbey Cwmhir the road descends uneventfully to Crossgates and the junction with the Rhayader road. Rhayader cannot be claimed as part of the border country, but most visitors will go through it sooner or later to reach the Elan Valley reservoir complex — highly recommended as a tour and certainly superior to Lake Vyrnwy as an attraction.

When the Corporation of Birmingham decided to buy the seventy square miles of the Elan and Claerwen valleys the plan was to build three reservoirs in each. The Elan scheme was completed and in use by 1904, but the plans for Claerwen were shelved until after the Second World War. Between 1946 and 1952 and 1000ft Claerwen dam was added to the complex and plans for the other two dams were abandoned.

The proximity of the Elan Valley has done much to sustain the popularity of our next stopping-place, Llandrindod Wells. You could never mistake Llandrindod for anything but a spa town. Its wide streets, elegant terraces, lawns and parks are unique in the border country. Llandrindod — the name means the Church of the Trinity — has had a stop-start history, unlike many spas that found themselves famous almost overnight. This may be the reason for its resilience; certainly it has not retreated into the shabby gentility that has been the fate of other watering-places.

There is evidence of the saline springs being used in the seventeenth century (the Romans probably appreciated them before that), but it was not until the middle of the eighteenth century that the waters were seriously exploited. In 1749, virtually at a stroke, a huge hotel was built overlooking the lake. It was designed as a fashionable social centre, and a rather incongruous one, being marooned in one of the least-populated areas of Britain. For a long time the hotel *was* the town, offering shops, sports and dances as well as highly-regarded standards of accommodation.

Unfortunately, the hotel also provided a suitably isolated venue for dubious weekends and discreditable gambling activities, and local opinion became firmly set against it. It closed in 1787, never having seriously made use of the healing waters. It was the arrival of the railway in 1865 and the emergence of the spa cult that gave the town a new lease of life. By the 1880s many thousands of visitors each year were coming to try the saline, sulphur, chalybeate and magnesium springs, and the status of Llandrindod had grown so rapidly that it became a meeting-place of the County Council. It is now the 'capital' of Powys and many of the County Council staff work in the old Pump House Hotel.

The waters have long since ceased to be a major attraction, and the town has developed as a centre for conferences and tourism. Nevertheless, its distinctive character justifies a detailed exploration, for which the obvious starting point is the Metropole Hotel, one of the most imposing buildings. It is an Edwardian structure, and its central block is typically gabled. Enlargement and modernisation has been successfully unified by the elegant full-length verandah. This gives the hotel a recognisable 'spa' appearance, enhanced by the pleasant garden opposite.

Next door to the Metropole and flanking the Memorial Gardens are the Town Hall and Museum, with, between them, a nostalgic survival of former days — an ornamental grotto made from a peculiar substance called tufa. Moving up Temple Street and turning left opposite a well-stocked bookshop you arrive at Middleton Street, a shopping centre which retains its own kind of dignity, being wide and free from heavy traffic. From the junction at the other end of Middleton Street two other notable hotels can be seen; the Glen Usk in South Crescent has some good iron-work, while the Commodore (formerly the rectory) is a splendid example of a Victorian urban mansion.

If you now go downhill and over the railway bridge there are some interesting arcaded shops in the demoted High Street, but dominating everything is the magnificent Victorian building of triangular design (formerly a hotel) now used as the District Council offices. To the left of this is Norton Terrace, which leads to one of Llandrindod's best-known features, the Rock Park.

The Park is a landscaped area of trees and paths with a stream running through, and at one end is the Pump Room, now restored to its former Betjemanesque eccentricity. In a dell in front of it, you can still find the tap providing free chalybeate water. Bowls enthusiasts will already be aware that Llandrindod is an international venue for the sport, and the extensive greens with fine hill views can be reached by walking up past the Pump Room.

The Radnor District Council has done much to refurbish the old public meeting-places and social centres. In Ithon Road, running down the other side of the District Council offices, is the Albert Hall, a rather severe former chapel. It is now an attractive theatre, thanks to Council grants and the efforts of local volunteers. As you re-cross the railway and walk down Spa Road you pass the Grand Pavilion, which has also been given a face-lift in order to turn it into a conference centre. Close by is the church hall, a misleading term because, like many other things in Llandrindod, it is on the grand scale.

At the bottom of Spa Road is the town's main garage, and it seems entirely fitting that it should be called the Automobile Palace, a name redolent of old Daimlers and Lagondas. There is, in fact, a collection of rather less glamorous vintage bicycles here. It is worth going straight up the hill opposite to look at the former Pump House Hotel, a fine early Victorian building on the site of one of the original springs. It is now the County Hall, and it is nice to see that the Planning Department has been accommodated in the most eccentric wing.

The road behind the Automobile Palace brings you to the lake, formed artificially in 1870 and perhaps a little overrated as a scenic feature. Somehow it never appears other than a grey expanse of featureless water, although there is compensation in the cheerful cafe serving good coffee. It is possible to walk round the lake, visiting on the way the original parish church, noted as the place where the first Archbishop of the

Church in Wales was formally elected in 1920.

This description of Llandrindod conveys little of its atmosphere, which is still that of a town with its own way of life, standing aloof from the surrounding countryside. It has none of the agricultural preoccupations of the other border towns, and its attraction for the visitor today is still what it was in the eighteenth century — a centre of 'civilised' life in an area which is beautiful but rugged. It encourages the quieter pleasures like bowls, fishing and walking, and there are indeed some good walks in the neighbourhood.

One which takes in many features of interest to the east of the town begins at the 'Old Church' of St Michael, easily reached from the lake road. It was Llandrindod's parish church until dismissed as inadequate in the nineteenth century. In order to persuade the stubborn congregation to use the new Holy Trinity Church in town the roof of St Michael's was removed. This led to such an outcry that the church was restored in 1875 — an odd story of a very expensive mistake.

After following the lane west of the church, pass the golf clubhouse, turn left and skirt the Little Hill. Pass along the top of the conifer plantation and then turn north to reach the track leading to Shaky Bridge. There is a forest trail here (leaflet from the Information Office) and immediately above is the site of Cefnllys Castle. There is a way back by lanes via Bailey Einion.

Cefnllys is of some interest because until 1885 it returned a Member of Parliament; in fact it was until then one of only six parliamentary boroughs in Radnorshire. It gained its status in Tudor times, and its administrative centre — the Court Leet — was at the nearby farmhouse of Neuadd. By 1832

4½
**

the electorate of Cefnllys numbered about half a dozen and there were only three houses of any size.

If you wish to visit another local landmark, the Alpine Bridge, you can do so by crossing Shaky Bridge (perfectly safe now), walking to the left around Cefnllys Castle Hill and joining the lane at Neuadd. Turn left at Cwm and follow the road to the bridge. There is a path and lane back to town on the other side. The main attraction here is the gorge cut by the river through the rock, and the spot is noted for its bird and plant life. The walk adds three miles to the previous one.

The old parish church is also the start of a longer walk to the east. Proceed as for the Shaky Bridge walk as far as GR 080604, where instead of turning left you follow the main track past Carregwiber Bank and then on to the plantation at Bwlch-llwyn Bank. Walk down the west side of the plantation and take the path that branches left at GR 116590. This is clearly shown on the map and leads back to the starting-point.

Finally, and for a change of scene, it is possible to walk south to Disserth and Newbridge. Turn off the A483 at GR 056600, cross the railway bridge, take the path almost immediately on the left and then cross the course of the old Roman Road. The path leads to an isolated farm (Llan-yr-Ithon) and after that it is marked clearly on the map. You enter Disserth at the river bridge and the church is close by. It is well worth a visit because it has remained largely unchanged since the seventeenth century; its notable features are the box pews and the three-decker pulpit.

Newbridge is reached either by continuing on the main road or by taking a short cut across the fields from Disserth bridge. It is a celebrated angling centre on the Wye, but is a

pleasant spot for the non-fisherman, too. From this direction you come into the village past the picturesque New Inn, turn right and then left to get to the river.

Whether you made the diversion to Disserth and Newbridge or not, the next major stopping-place is Builth Wells. The Revd. Francis Kilvert is on record in his diary as saying 'a beautiful enchantment hangs over Builth and the town is magically transformed still'. He was thinking particularly of the huddle of slate roofs, but it takes a certain effort of the imagination to summon up a sense of enchantment in a town as severely practical as Builth. There is no frivolity here; an asphalt car park has been laid on the one area that might have been transformed into riverside gardens, and the nearest thing to festivity is the Royal Welsh Show, held annually on a permanent site across the river.

The origins of the town lie in the fact that there was an important ford here, and a succession of castles has been sited on the high ground opposite the crossing-point. It was near here that Llewlyn ap Gruffydd, the last native Prince of Wales, was killed in 1282 after fleeing from Edward I's army in North Wales — tradition has it that he was refused refuge in Builth Castle.

In addition to having this death on their consciences the townsfolk have encountered other major misfortunes. The Black Death was especially severe here, and in 1691 a disastrous fire destroyed virtually the whole town. An effort to promote Builth as a spa in the 1830s was a short-lived success, owing to the poor access and the distance of the pump-room from the town. Since then the inhabitants seem to have made up their minds to live unobtrusively and not to tempt providence with any further imaginative enterprises.

Even the Wye can do little to enliven the scene. The fact that this was once a ford indicates that the river is normally placid here, and even in flood it merely takes on a sullen air, whereas a little further downstream it foams and leaps excitingly. The six-arched bridge constructed in 1779 and widened in 1925, stands precisely at a right-angled bend in the river. At its southern end is the market hall, easily the town's most attractive building, and now housing the Wyeside Arts Centre as well. The basement room, almost at river level, is probably unique in being both a public market and a concert hall, while upstairs there is a pleasant little auditorium and art gallery.

The castle mound lies above the bridge but is on private ground and not normally accessible. High Street, with most of the shops and a pleasantly varied assortment of homely

The Market Hall and Arts Centre, Builth Wells

architecture, runs up from the bridge towards the church. There is an odd conglomeration of styles, combining a massive fourteenth-century tower with a Victorian nave and chancel. The restorers failed to transfer much from the previous church, apart from an effigy of John Lloyd, servant to Elizabeth I, which was placed, possibly as an afterthought, in the porch.

Builth has something of the atmosphere of a quarry town, and indeed the Llanelwedd quarries are visible from the bridge. Much of the stone for the Elan Valley reservoir construction came from here, and the hillsides are still worked today, though mainly for roadstone. The other main economic factor in the town's life is, of course, agriculture. It is reflected in the range of shops, and there is a lively cattle market on Mondays.

This is a suitable place to mention the Wye Valley Walk, a 36 mile waymarked path from Rhayader to Hay-on-Wye. Although the main road follows the river closely south of Builth Wells you get a very inadequate view of it because the side of the road is thickly wooded. The Wye Valley Walk takes you over much higher ground with magnificent views of the valley from the western side. When you see the Aberedw Rocks high above the river six miles below Builth, you may feel like crossing to investigate further.

According to legend, Llewelyn ap Gruffydd came to Aberedw while being pursued by Edward I's men and hired a local blacksmith to reverse the shoes on his horse, so that the tracks he made would appear to be leading in the opposite direction. He spent the night in a cave among the Rocks (it can still be seen) but was betrayed by the blacksmith and had to flee. After his unsuccessful attempt to get refuge in

Builth Castle, he and his men were killed close by. A large stone commemorating the event can be seen by the road at the neighbouring hamlet of Cilmery.

A short distance downstream is Erwood, which nowadays has a bridge, although for centuries it was a famous fording-place. This is where Llewelyn's enemies crossed in search of him, and many years later it was the favourite crossing-place for the Welsh drovers on their way to England. Many hair-raising stories have survived of their efforts to get cattle across when the Wye was in flood. Erwood has another, unexpected, claim to fame. When the London writer Henry Mayhew was forced to escape his creditors for a while, he lodged here at the house which is now the village shop. It was while he was having a quiet drink in the Erwood Inn that the idea of founding a humorous magazine occured to him, and so 'Punch' was born.

The old drover's road from Erwood is now the B4594, and it is still a good way to start an exploration of the Radnor 'interior'. Almost as soon as you start, there is a desirable diversion; two miles from Erwood a turn to the right takes you to the falls at Craig Pwll Du. About three miles further on at Llanbach Howey another lane to the south gives access to a whole jumble of tracks around the Begwns, and the summit (at nearly 1400 feet) can be reached quite easily by following the map.

By this time the nature of this remarkably remote countryside becomes clear; to the right of the road there is a network of navigable lanes into the Wye Valley, but they stop at the road, and the area to the left is crossed only by tracks and paths. Painscastle is the first village of any size along the road. It was once an important town, fought over several times, and Henry III had his court here for a short time. Nothing survives of the

4½
**

castle, although the defensive earthworks are still in evidence to the south of the village. It was here that the drovers branched off to head for the Rhydspence Inn (see chapter 6)

The lane leading north from Painscastle is the starting-point for several long rambles in the hills. One possible objective is Red Hill (GR 157501) standing at 1600 feet. The best route is around the west side. A return can be made via Hondon and Llettypeod. Another challenging hill is Colva (GR 195554), visible to the north from the road and reached by a lane (GR 203493) just over two miles beyond Rhosgoch. Other routes abound on the map, but good equipment, including a compass, is advised. Rhosgoch Common, incidentally, is an expanse of a marsh of some interest to botanists.

Newchurch, at the junction of three river valleys, is one of the best bases for walking in the area, offering everything from a gentle stroll to a strenuous all-day ramble. It is the first major settlement on the river Arrow, which

becomes so important further east. You meet the Offa's Dyke path again here and can use it to walk the four miles to Gladestry. Part of the path is indicated on the latest OS map, but the start of the section is just to the north of Newchurch bridge, and it passes over Disgwylfa Hill between the two ponds.

Gladestry is at the end of the Hergest Ridge, described in chapter 6, and the Ridgeway makes a fine walk into Kington. There is also a rather easier route to Colva Hill by way of the lane running west out of the village. If you stay on the B4594 you run into an extensive limestone quarrying area where the minor roads are not quite as clear as they appear on the map. It is best to go to the junction with the A44, which gives a chance to stop and look at the impressive Stanner Rocks. Turn left here and then left again at Walton in order to reach Old Radnor.

This tiny settlement is another example of an early village being abandoned in favour of a 'planned' town nearby. Old Radnor church, however,

Offa's Dyke

remains famous. It is in an elevated position (one of the few churches with a compelling view from its windows) and is full of treasures inside. The tub font attracts attention at once; it is pre-Norman and said to be the largest in Britain. The wide rood screen is superb, but the unique feature of the church is the organ case of linen-fold panelling dating from the sixteenth century.

You return to the main road and turn left for New Radnor, a large village with its church set up high among the trees and its roads still tracing out the early medieval ground plan. There is nothing left of its once formidable castle, but remains of the old town walls survive on the southern edge of the village.

Here we are on the border of that convoluted mass of hills that make up the Radnor Forest. Roads run all round it, but any exploration of the Forest itself must be on foot. Bache Hill, one of the highest in the Forest, is accessible by way of the lane leading north past the castle site. Follow it until it becomes a path at the south-western corner of a plantation. Follow the path past the Whinyard Rocks to the next plantation; then walk along the southern edge of this to GR 224640. A track leads south-

7½
**

west into the plantation at GR 210628. Follow it east to Ferndale, then south-west to Knowle Hill, and back into New Radnor.

A shorter walk can be taken to the famous falls known as Water-break-its-neck. You leave the A44 two miles south-west of New Radnor at GR 195593 and follow the lane into the Warren plantation. The falls are about eighty feet high and fall into a dark

2½
*

PLACES OF INTEREST IN THE RADNOR FOREST

Old Radnor Church
Exceptional font, rood screen and organ case.

Water-break-its-neck, waterfall, 3m west of New Radnor

The Pales, 1m north of Llandegley Old Quaker meeting house.

Burfa Camp, 4m south-west of Presteigne
Very large hill fort. Various other earthworks in the area.

The village of New Radnor

6½
**

ravine, but don't expect anything spectacular during a dry spell. You can make a complete circuit round the Mynd by carrying on south-west and then taking the track south-east to Llanfihangel-nant-Melan.

8
***

Another popular ramble is up the Harley Dingle to Shepherd's Well — access is at GR 204605. ('Dingle' is misleading, because it is more of a

*

ravine.) For a gentle stroll there are various paths on the Smatcher, reached by the lane at GR 216606.

The next stop along the A44 should be at Llandegley. It is an interesting village for two reasons. First, it is a miniature spa, with saline, sulphur and chalybeate springs. In the middle ages it attracted pilgrims suffering from a type of epilepsy called St Tegla's disease. The Well House can still be seen in a field near the village centre. Its other notable feature is the isolated seventeenth-century Quaker meeting-house known

3
*

as The Pales. It is a mile or so to the north, and can be reached by car, but it makes a good walk, starting at GR 136631 and going north-west to meet the lane half a mile west of The Pales. The circuit can be completed by joining the minor road leading due south and turning right on to a path at GR 141638.

2
**

The walk up to the Llandegley Rocks should not be missed. It is a straightforward route, clear on the map and starting at the churchyard.

The route round the Radnor Forest continues with a right turn on to the A488 at Penybont. Llanfihangel Rhydithon, three miles later, looks over the Aran valley and has its back to some of the wildest country in Radnor. It is the access point for a notable track that crosses the Forest range completely and finishes at Water-break-its-neck.

7½
**

Various circular walks can be planned by branching from it; one of the most popular begins at GR 165637 and goes north-east to a plantation with the Rhiw Pool on its northern edge. The return is via Old Hall at GR 164667.

At the Rhiw Pool, there is an alternative track leading to Bleddfa. Its name means literally 'The Place of the Wolves' — sufficient indication of its former remoteness. (Apparently the last wolf in the Radnor Forest was killed in the sixteenth century.) Like many other settlements Bleddfa suffered at the hands of Owain Glyndwr, whose men burned the church tower in 1401, and this incident was vividly substantiated when excavation in the late 1960s revealed the blackened remains of the tower. They can now be seen next to the church. An interesting feature of the interior is the roof, which retains some of the original painted colouring on its timbers. The church is now in the care of a local Trust, whose members aim to restore it fully, not only as a place of worship but as a cultural centre.

2½
*

A lane north-west from Bleddfa through Dolaney Farm leads to the attractive St Michael's Pool. The walk can be extended by taking another lane

3
*

north-east from the Pool to the village of Llangunllo, standing near the source of the river Lugg. It is an impressive situation, surrounded by hills, and perhaps the most surprising thing about it is the fact that it has a railway station some way to the north. At the time of writing the trains still stop there.

From Bleddfa the A488 moves on to cross the Lugg and to reach a junction with the B4356. At this point you are bound to notice the large gaunt house standing by the road. It is Elizabethan and unusual in being stone-built, but it appears to be deteriorating rapidly — altogether a sad and rather eerie sight. Its name — Monaughty — looks Irish, but in fact it is a corruption of the Welsh

'Mynach-dy', 'The Place of the Monk'. The explanation is that when Abbey Cwmhir was dissolved, the Abbot retired to one of the community's farms, the site of which can be seen by the river a mile towards Llangunllo.

Having turned on to the B4356, you pass, within a mile, the site of the battle of Pilleth, when Owain Glyndwr defeated and slaughtered an English army composed mainly of Herefordshire men under Sir Edmund Mortimer. The battle is referred to with grisly implications at the beginning of *'Henry IV, Part One'*. Pilleth had become famous before this as a place of pilgrimage for people hoping to be relieved by the waters of a nearby well, said to be particularly effective for eye disease. The church, virtually rebuilt in the 1890s, stands isolated above the battlefield, and from this direction you will need to watch carefully for the entrance through Pilleth Court. There is a circular walk starting and finishing at Pilleth Court and encircling Graig Hill.

There is now no reason to stop before Presteigne, a placid town right on the border (in fact on the 'wrong' side of Offa's Dyke). Despite this, it was until fairly recently the county town of Radnorshire, and some of its buildings reflect this former importance. The most striking is undoubtedly the Radnorshire Arms, a seventeenth-century black and white inn whose unusually large and inviting porch has protruding steps. The Duke's Arms, boasting a galleried yard, rivals it in interest. Another of Presteigne's gems is the early nineteenth-century Shire Hall, an elegant building in a vaguely classical style but fitting well into the proportions of the town.

The church is mainly fourteenth century, and its greatest treasure is a magnificent sixteenth-century Flemish tapestry. It is from here that the curfew rings every evening, a custom almost unique in Britain now. The rest of the town centre is mainly in a quiet Georgian style, providing an air of restful solidity. Presteigne was once a busy, main road town; it is now a backwater, but if any of the inhabitants regret this, they should take a look at Kington, which now carries the traffic instead.

There are some attractive walks to the south. A lane leading out through the Warden, the public space around the castle site, continues below Harley's Hill. If you branch left at GR 288644 and turn left again after a few hundred yards, you can make the return through a plantation and back into the town by way of Paradise Farm.

PLACES OF INTEREST IN AND AROUND KNIGHTON

Offa's Dyke
Particularly impressive stretches to the north of Knighton, especially on Llanfair Hill.

Offa's Dyke Association Centre, The old primary school, West Street Displays giving background information about the Dyke. Wide variety of literature available on the Dyke path and other local walks.

Just two miles west of Presteigne on the B4362 is Dolley Green, and the Offa's Dyke path passes across the road close to the village, at GR 278656. You can go down off the road here, across the river footbridge and get on to the Dyke at GR 273651. It is a steep climb but a rewarding one, and the waymarked path goes on to Ditchyeld. A glance at the map will show that this is an area of great archaeological interest.

This last walk can be turned into a circular one by turning off the Dyke path at GR 275631, taking the lane to Thorn and then the minor road to Discoed. To the south-east of Presteigne is the fine woodland area known as Wapley Hill, with a hill fort in the middle. Walks of various lengths are possible here — the best access points are on the southern side.

The B4355 north from Presteigne is the road to Knighton. On the way you pass through the large and attractive village of Norton, which, as the name implies, was a Saxon settlement. The church, which by all accounts was rather run down in the early nineteenth century, is a good example of sympathetic restoration by the distinguished architect Sir Giles Gilbert Scott. He rebuilt the bell turret in the original style and restored the fine rood screen, using much of the original carving.

The enlightened squire who had the work done in 1868 was Sir Richard Green-Price, who was also responsible for bringing rail communications to Radnorshire. It was Sir Richard who planted a grove of trees on the spot where a large number of human bones were disinterred near Pilleth — they were presumed to be those of the English soldiers killed in the battle.

There is a monument to Sir Richard, and it can be included in an interesting walk to the west of Norton. It starts on the road opposite the churchyard gate. Walk to GR 298670, and then branch north through the wood. The track leads along a ridge and joins the B4355. Turn left just before this road to reach the monument. You can go on to join the Dyke path at GR 284686, which goes south to GR 284674. Turn left here on to a track which returns to Norton.

And so to Knighton, which has some claim to be *the* border town, since it is right on Offa's Dyke and has some of the finest stretches on the hills to either side. Not surprisingly it is the headquarters of the Offa's Dyke

The Square, Knighton

Association, and your first visit should be to their centre at the old primary school in West Street. Here you can obtain a wealth of information and inexpensive literature about the Dyke, its path and various other walks in the district. One of the Association's most useful publications is the booklet of notes providing almost a yard-by-yard guide to the long-distance path. It is intended for use with the special strip maps, but is just as valuable when used with the ordinary OS map. It will certainly come in handy even if you walk only short stretches of the path.

There is nothing particularly remarkable about Knighton itself. It has much in common with Oswestry and Kington as a town serving the needs of agriculture and a scattered rural population. The most obvious feature is a clock tower of a kind which seems to have been a Victorian status symbol — Rhayader and Hay have them, as have several other Welsh towns. The double-naved church is unpretentious, and there are some interesting buildings tucked away, but most visitors will find Knighton attractive as a centre for walking, riding and fishing.

The final section of this tour is to the north-west of Knighton up the Teme valley. The route is the B4355 (easy to miss in the town — signposted 'Newtown'). The first village is Knucklas, which boasts an unexpectedly grandiose railway viaduct. It is a tiny place now, but resembled Cefnllys in being a fully-fledged borough represented in Parliament until 1885. Its near-neighbour on the road, Llanfair Waterdine, has a particularly fine length of Dyke above it, accessible by way of a lane north of the village. Equally worthwhile is the walk to Beacon Hill to the west of the road. There are many routes to it, but the most direct way is via the track starting at Pennant Pound (GR 216773). At 2000 feet, this is one of the highest points in the Radnor area.

Beguildy is spelt thus on the map, but originally it was Bugeildy — 'The Shepherd's House'. It is a final reminder of the contribution that the Radnor, Clun and Kerry Forests have made to sheep farming, including the introduction of two distinct breeds. Beguildy church is yet another that was remote enough to escape the 'reformers' and consequently retained its intricate fourteenth-century rood screen. The pulpit and altar are Jacobean.

Between Beguildy and Felindre, there are a multitude of paths and tracks leading into the hills to the south. After Felindre the road, which has hitherto been fairly level, starts to climb steeply up to Kerry Hill, providing final spectacular views over the Clun Forest. Three miles before joining the A483 at Dolfor, you pass Cider House Farm, the starting-point for the Kerry Ridgeway walk described in chapter 4. The last part of the journey is a gradual winding descent into Newtown.

6 Ludlow, Leominster and West Herefordshire

This chapter is devoted to three important border towns and some of the countryside which they serve. Ludlow, Leominster and Hereford form a vertical line on the map, creating a natural boundary to this part of the border region, where the landscape is very different from the deserted uplands of Radnor. Here we have pastoral valleys, rich agricultural land and picturesque villages — very much a lived-in landscape and yet strongly influenced historically by the proximity of Wales.

For many people Ludlow is the perfect town, with fine castle ruins, one of England's largest parish churches, a pleasing mixture of architecture, a river setting and a bustling social and cultural life. Others find it a little too self-conscious and 'arty', compared with other border towns, but no-one can deny its attractions.

It is set defensively inside a bend of the river Teme with the tributary river Corve guarding its north-west side, and the old town to the west of the A49 preserves the grid pattern of a typical medieval settlement. The castle has a very close relationship with the town, symbolised by the old market square just outside the castle gates, and the whole of this central area is a cosy huddle of crowded buildings and narrow streets.

Ludlow's origins are obscure, but there was a developing community here at the end of the twelfth century with an economy based on the local wool trade, and like many wool towns its wealth was demonstrated in the size of its parish church. In the early fourteenth century the manor passed to the powerful Mortimer family, and when Edward IV (a Mortimer) was crowned king, Ludlow became a royal retreat. At various times the castle accommodated Edward V and his brother (the 'princes in the Tower'), Mary Tudor and Prince Arthur, the short-lived son of Henry VII. Arthur brought his bride Catherine of Aragon here. It is hardly surprising that, when Henry VII set up a Council of the Marches to govern Wales and the border, Ludlow was chosen as its headquarters.

In the eighteenth and nineteenth centuries, the town became the centre of a fashionable social scene, with two theatres and a racecourse, and it was during this period that the elegant Georgian houses were built. The annual Arts Festival still recaptures some of this atmosphere, and the recently-completed by-pass has brought back to Ludlow something of its old tranquillity.

A tour of the town should start at Castle Square, which was originally one end of a broad main street from the castle gates to the Bull Ring beyond the church. Medieval building (and the nineteenth-century market hall) converted this street into a series of narrow lanes. The castle stands on a precipice falling away to the river and has a huge outer bailey, part of which consists of private gardens. The entrance to the inner bailey is through an Elizabethan gateway by the intimidating keep, which still has many of its interior features. The most striking building in the inner bailey is the round twelfth-century chapel, dedicated to St Mary Magdelene and revealing some fine

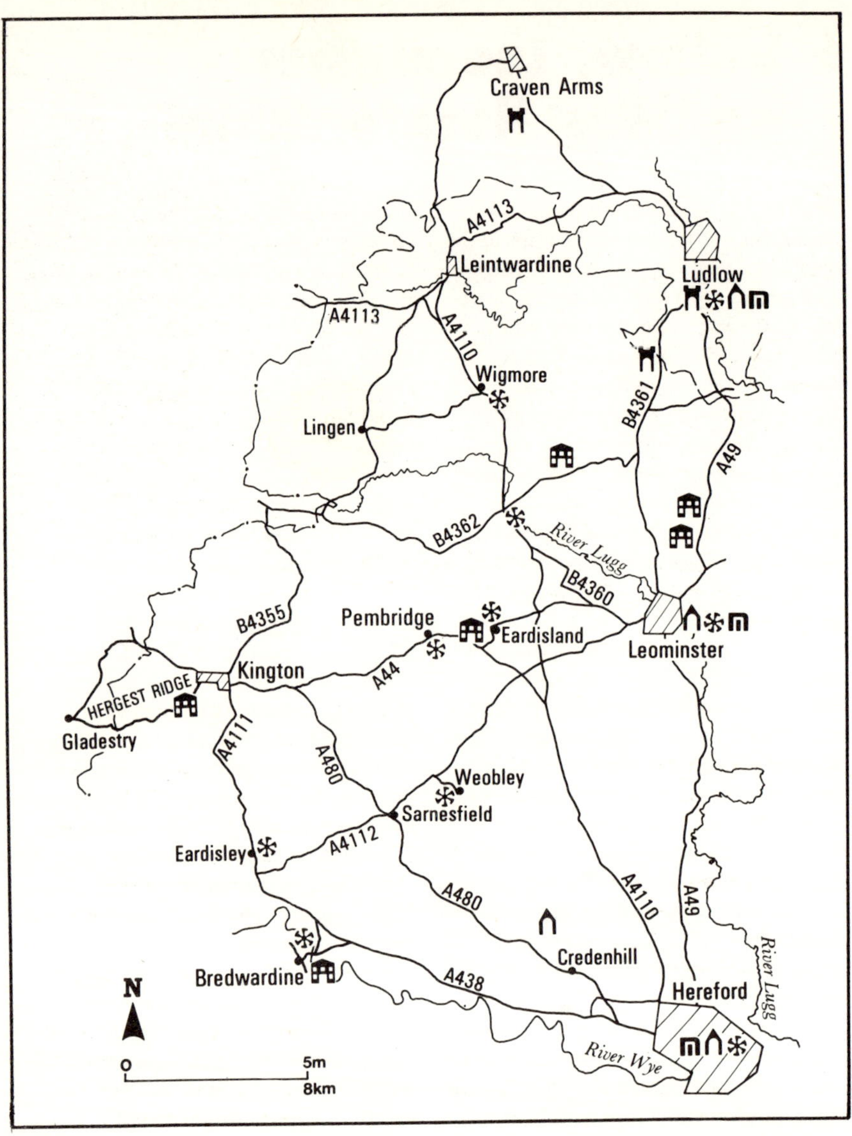

Norman decoration. Beyond the chapel is a well-preserved range of domestic buildings; they include the Great Hall, the scene of the first performance of Milton's 'Comus' in 1634. On each side of the Hall are residential quarters where the royal visitors mentioned earlier must have lived.

It is a short walk along the High Street to St Laurence's church. On the way, you pass the Buttermarket, erected in 1746. Its upper floor was for some time a schoolroom, and it now houses the town museum. On the corner of Broad Street nearby is a fine group of fifteenth-century buildings. Before entering the

A characteristic mixture of architectural styles in Ludlow

church it is worth walking round the churchyard to see the thirteenth-century Reader's House and the grave of A E Housman, a Worcestershire man buried in the place that features so often in his poems.

After passing through the hexagonal porch — an almost unique feature — you become aware at once of the cathedral-like proportions of the church, but what immediately catches the attention is the superb east window and the elaborate reredos beneath it. There is no space here for a detailed description of St Laurence's — the excellent town guidebook does this well enough — but if you have time for only a quick visit you should not miss the highly individual misericords in the choir stalls or the north chancel chapel of the ancient Palmers' Guild, which has some magnificent stained glass.

In contrast to the closely-packed buildings of the High Street, Broad Street is a spacious and elegant thoroughfare, with the Angel — a traditional coaching inn — standing out among the harmonious frontages. Running parallel to it from the castle gates is Mill Street, containing the Guildhall and the old Grammar School. If you turn left just beyond the school and walk through to the Broadgate you can continue on via St John's Road and emerge into Old Street, part of an ancient Roman road. On the slope down towards the river there is a row of small terraced houses that are an object lesson in the incorporation of modern development into an ancient town.

At the top of Old Street is the congested junction known as the Bull Ring, and just past it stands the Feathers Hotel, featured on so many calendars and probably the best-known building in Ludlow. Built in 1603 it has an incredible profusion of decorative carving and an inviting balcony. But do not miss the Bull on the other side of the road — not so spectacular, but considerably older.

On the other side of the Teme bridge there is a minor road to the right signposted 'Whitecliffe'. This leads to the common, where the town's cattle grazed in the middle ages. Now it is a public area, wooded and with any number of walks. About a mile and a half along the road, you will find the Mortimer Forest Museum, with displays of forest lore and wildlife. From here it is possible with the aid of a map to walk to Leintwardine, seven miles west of Ludlow and the starting point for a tour which samples the attractions of north Herefordshire. The quick way round for the motorist is via the A49 north of Ludlow, turning left at Bromfield.

Leintwardine (the Roman settlement of Bravonium) is a long, thin village, stretched out alongside the road. Nowadays it is mainly of interest to fishermen, being at the confluence of the Teme and Clun. The church is of interest because it is built on the old Roman defence works, with the result that the chancel is much higher than the nave. Less than a mile from Leintwardine you branch left on to the A4110 and soon come to Adforton, where a left turn will bring you to Wigmore Abbey. It was established in 1179. Some traces remain but the site is now on private land and can be viewed only with permission.

Soon after Adforton the wooded hills on the right reveal an impressive castle mound and ruins, the first indication of the attractive village of Wigmore. Perhaps 'town' would be more appropriate because it was the administrative centre of northern Herefordshire for a long time, and its wide main street still gives it an air of importance. The oddest feature of this street is certainly the sight of a genuine half-timbered building next to what looks like a half-timbered Nissen hut housing the village stores. At the top of the street a lane leads up beside an interesting, solitary brick house to the church. It is a spacious structure, with floors on different levels and with a particularly fine pulpit. A short distance to the west is an early motte and bailey, the predecessor of the much bigger castle on the outskirts, which can be visited only by appointment with the owners of the land.

There is some fine hill and forest country around here, and one way to see it is to turn right just past Wigmore and take the undulating road to Lingen. When you reach the woodland, there are plenty of opportunities for short strolls on the forest tracks.

A longer walk begins about half a mile beyond the crossroads called 'Cross of the Tree'. It is signposted as a public footpath and leads away to the right of the road along an escarpment overlooking the river valley. When the path meets a metalled road turn left and then right after half a mile on to a lane that takes you to the top of Harley's Mountain. A path due south then brings you on to the road into Lingen.

In Lingen itself there is a motte and bailey tucked away behind the farm at Court House, and the church has some interesting sixteenth-century pews, said to have come from the nearby convent at Limebrook. Turning south at the road junction in Lingen you pass a turning to the remains of the convent after a mile. It was never a big community, but the nuns were extensive landowners before the Dissolution in 1539. Another mile brings you to the river Lugg at Kinsham. Just before the bridge is the start of a riverside walk, of optional length, through the gorge which the river has cut.

The short route to the B4362 is through Byton, but it is worth following

6½
**

*

Genuine and false half-timber at Wigmore

the signs for Presteigne and joining the main road at Combe, because, after turning left, you pass beneath the superb wooded ridge of Wapley Hill, which is particularly beautiful in the autumn.

Shobdon, the first village you come to on the B4362, is a scattered place with a large caravan park and an airfield. Apart from these it is noted for its unusual mock-Gothic church, built in 1752 to replace a Norman church. Some remains of the original were re-erected nearby as a sort of folly. Mortimer's Cross is the site of a decisive battle of the Wars of the Roses in 1461. It was a triumph for Edward, Duke of York, who was crowned as Edward IV a few months later. The local pub sign shows the red and white roses and also three suns, commemorating a trick of the light on the frosty day of the battle. The main attraction here now is a water-driven flour mill, a few hundred yards up the Aymstrey road.

You are recommended to cross the A4110 and continue on the B4362 to reach an area of particular interest. Three miles after Mortimer's Cross is a left turn for Croft Castle, one of the few great houses in these parts open to the public. It is basically a fifteenth-century fortified mansion overlaid with later Gothic 'improvements', including a facade providing a false top storey. Inside there are some fine paintings and good furniture, some by Chippendale.

It is a short walk from the rear of the castle to Croft Ambrey, the hill fort on a commanding spur overlooking the Wigmore area. The walk can be extended rewardingly by going east along the edge of the wood and then south on to Bircher Common, now National Trust property. The views throughout the walk are superb.

After this diversion, the road continues through the pleasant village of Bircher to join the B4361, and if you turn left you arrive at the first of several lanes leading to Orleton. There is a timber-framed manor house here where the poet Pope once stayed and a Norman church with a particularly fine carved font. The final stop before re-entering Ludlow is at Richard's Castle. The modern village by the road is undistinguished and the visitor needs to travel a mile up a side road to the west to see the site of one of the very earliest Norman castles, probably founded before the Conquest by Richard le Scrob, who gave his name to the village. Nearby is the old church, rarely used now, with a detached tower and seventeenth-century box pews.

Anyone who prefers to walk back to Ludlow can start about a mile and a half further on from Richard's Castle. There is a lay-by, with a track off to the left leading up to Whitecliffe, where this tour started.

To explore the central border area of Herefordshire it is best to start at Leominster (pronounced 'Lemster'). On the way there from Ludlow there are two interesting houses open to the public. They lie within a mile of each other off the A49, and are reached by a turning to the right three miles after Brimfield. The first, Berrington Hall, is National Trust property and stands in an extensive park laid out by Capability Brown. It was built during the period 1778-1781 for Thomas Harley, a former Lord Mayor of London. Its severe, rectangular exterior contains a wealth of elegant decoration and furnishing inside. The showpiece of the house is the staircase hall, a masterpiece by the architect Henry Holland.

Eye Manor was built in 1680 as a retirement home for Ferdinando Gorges, a Barbados merchant who made a fortune out of slaves and sugar. Once

The Priory Church, Leominster

again you should not judge the house by its rather modest exterior, because inside there is some highly exotic decoration, including a good deal of remarkable plasterwork. The present owners have added considerably to the attractions of the house with displays of books from Mr Sandford's Golden Cockerel Press and of corn dollies, one of Mrs Sandford's interests. Period costumes, needlework and costume dolls are also on show.

One must beware of being trapped in Leominster's one-way system, and you should take advantage of the large car park on the left soon after you enter the town from the north. As a town, Leominster has been overshadowed by its grander neighbours, Ludlow and Hereford, but many visitors will find its intimate atmosphere and general homeliness more appealing. In fact, it has much in common with its rivals, including a parish church on the grand

Folk Museum, Etnam Street
Displays of local life in the past.

Dinmore Manor, near Westhope,
adjacent to Queenswood Country
Park
Sixteenth-century building with
additions, chapel of Knights of St
John of Jerusalem.

The Grange, in park adjacent to
churchyard
Former town hall by John Abel, now
local government offices. One of the
finest half-timbered buildings in the
county.

Berrington Hall, off A49, 4m north of
Leominster
Eighteenth-century mansion with
much original decoration and fine
furniture. Dairy and Victorian
laundry, gardens.

Eye Manor, off A49, 4m north of
Leominster
Plain exterior hides exotic interior.
Impressive seventeenth-century
plasterwork. Special displays —
books, china, costumes, corn-dollies

Burton Court, Eardisland, 6m west of
Leominster
Eighteenth-century house with
nineteenth-century additions.
Fourteenth-century Great Hall.
Special displays — period costume,
fairground models etc. Soft fruit farm
— pick your own in season.

Croft Castle, on B4362, 4m north-
west of Leominster
Walls and fortifications of fourteenth
and fifteenth centuries. Main house
of sixteenth century with 'Gothic'
additions. Fine grounds.

Burford House Gardens, 1m west of
Tenbury Wells (north-east of
Leominster)
Famous gardens and nurseries
producing rare and unusual plants.
Plants for sale.

Watermill, Mortimer Cross, short
distance along Aymstrey road
Eighteenth century mill, last used in
1940.

Priory church
Large, unique church of outstanding
architectural interest. Scolds'
ducking stool.

---

scale, a medieval centre and some good
Georgian architecture.

It is the latter that first becomes
noticeable as you approach the town
centre from the car park. Broad Street
lives up to its name, and has some
pleasing eighteenth-century buildings
that function in an unassuming way as
shops and offices. At the top of Broad
Street you reach the heart of the old
town, with a wealth of timber-framed
buildings in High Street and Draper's

Lane. Much of the ancient beauty of
these buildings has been lost at ground
level because of the modernisation of
shop-fronts, but the first floors show a
fascinating variety of styles.

Corn Square, at the other end of
Draper's Lane, is the site of the town's
open-air market, and beyond is Etnam
Street, containing a mixture of Georgian
and timber-framed architecture. A small
folk museum has been established here.
The building it occupies was once a

The Grange, Leominster

mission hall for navvies.

Church Street leads off from the top of Broad Street, displaying some handsome eighteenth and nineteenth-century houses. It takes you to the Priory Church, which is not only a unique building in itself but a reminder that the town's origins were ecclesiastical. The first religious community was probably founded here in about 660 and was the spiritual centre for a very wide area before Hereford Cathedral was built to take over that role. Successive communities did not run smoothly, and in 1123 Leominster Priory was put under the jurisdiction of

Reading Abbey.

It was at this time that work was begun on rebuilding the Priory Church, and the 'Norman nave' is readily identifiable by its massive pillars and the fact that it is on a lower level than the rest of the church. An aisle on its left contains, rather incongruously, the town's ducking stool for scolds. This original portion was dedicated to St Peter, whereas the central nave, built in 1239 for the benefit of the townspeople, is dedicated to St Paul. To the south is a huge aisle which is virtually a third nave. It was added in 1320 in the elegant 'decorated' style, with a set of

Eardisland

magnificent windows. Originally the church was about twice its present length, but the choir, presbytery and Lady Chapel, which made up the east end, were destroyed at the Reformation.

There is one other important building in Leominster, reached by going south through the churchyard gate into the neighbouring park. It is now called the Grange and accommodates local authority offices. In 1633, however, it was erected at the top of Broad Street as the town hall, with an open ground floor for use as a market. The builder was John Abel, Herefordshire's master-craftsman in timber-framing, whose name will occur again later. It was moved to its present site in 1853, and although the ground floor has now been filled in it remains one of the county's best traditional buildings.

The route out of Leominster for a tour of the Arrow valley is the A44, and the first stop is at Eardisland. If a Hollywood set-designer had been given the task of creating an English village he would probably have come up with something like Eardisland. An old bridge spans a narrow river whose banks are immaculate lawns. Gleaming black-and-white cottages group themselves picturesquely around it, a mellow brick dove-cot is in the middle distance and a mill stream winds its way through. Only the thatch is missing.

It is rather a relief to find that you pass a muddy farm to get to the church and that the church is not exceptional, apart from a fine modern stained-glass window showing Christ as the Good Shepherd with black-and-white houses in the background. The manor house behind the dove-cot has had a recent face-lift, but the same cannot be said for the village's most interesting building — Staick House — which stands rather

94

forlornly on the other side of the bridge. Its oldest section is fourteenth century, and extensions were built in the two succeeding centuries. Its roof is a good example of sandstone slab cladding.

A turning to the left after the bridge will bring you to Burton Court, which is open to the public. It is mainly late eighteenth century with later additions, among them a porch by Clough Williams Ellis of Portmeirion fame. The oldest part of the house is a fourteenth-century Great Hall. Extra interest is provided by a collection of models, curios and items of period costume. If you go at the right times, you can pick your own soft fruit and get a good tea afterwards.

PLACES OF INTEREST AROUND KINGTON

Penrhos Court, 4m east of Kington on A44
Fine timber-framed buildings, now a real ale brewery.

The Ley, Weobley
Outstanding Elizabethan timber-framed house with stone roof. Open by appointment only (see Further Information).

Hergest Croft Gardens, $2\frac{1}{2}$m west of Kington off A44
Arboretum, over 1000 varieties of trees, shrubs and flowers. Rare plants for sale.

Cwmmau Farmhouse, at Brilley, south-west of Kington
Typical Herefordshire farmhouse (Jacobean) preserved by National Trust. Occupied privately and open only be appointment, except on rare occasions (see Further Information).

As you walk from Eardisland bridge into the village there is a turning on the right marked 'Unsuitable for Heavy Vehicles'. It is the start of a pleasant walk via Folly Farm and Broom Farm into Pembridge. On the way you pass the former Pembridge station, now a private house.

Pembridge is equally picturesque but much less self-conscious. Its timber-framed houses are lined up solidly on each side of the road and few of them have been 'done up', so there is still a sense of the inhabitants leading normal working lives and refusing to become exhibits. The natural focus of the village is half-way along the main street, where the church, the market hall and the New Inn form an interesting group.

The inn is seventeenth century and perhaps over-restored, but the market hall, with its open ground floor, is of interest because the supporting timbers still show the notches that held the merchants' stalls in position over three hundred years ago. The steps to the churchyard are opposite, and it comes as a slight shock to be confronted with an almost grotesque detached belfry, squat and massive. It was obviously built to serve also as a fortress. By way of contrast, the church, rebuilt in the fourteenth century, has an atmosphere of elegance and richness, and its size is a reminder that Pembridge was once an important borough. As at Llansilin, near Oswestry, the scars on the west door are said to have been made by Civil War musketry.

A feature of Pembridge is the number of cruck houses. This form of building, in which the timbers are fastened to giant, curved As at each end of the house, is widespread in Herefordshire. The Forge and Victoria Place in East Street are examples.

The village of Lyonshall, just off the

main road a few miles on from Pembridge, is remarkable for being unremarkable — a pleasant, unpretentious place, where the craze for prettifying has had little effect. Rather more spectacular is Penrhos Court, just before Kington. It is a very big cruck house with associated buildings, and is now a brewery for real ale.

And so into Kington, which is in fact two towns. By a process common in the border country, the original settlement at the top of the hill has been outstripped by later development below it. The A44 enters at the less attractive end, and the first problem is finding the car park. Drive through the main street and carry straight on where the street turns right at a rather ugly Victorian market hall. The car park is a few yards along this side road (Mill Street).

Kington is like several towns we have encountered before in making no claim to be anything but a useful rural centre. A combination of narrow pavements and heavy lorries make it difficult to enjoy the little main street, and indeed there is not a great deal to see there. The Burton Arms, opposite the market hall mentioned earlier, is a remarkably attractive mid-Victorian building; behind the market hall a recent piece of restoration has produced the Old Coach House, built on brick piers and housing the public conveniences. Inexplicably, the tiny square next to it is called the Place des Marines.

The original part of the town, surrounding the church, has a good deal of interest. The church itself is large and built on a commanding site. The Norman tower has a distinctive three-decker spire and was once detached; it is still semi-detached. The rest of the church is something of a conglomeration of alterations and additions. The principal feature is the tomb in the south chancel of Thomas Vaughan and his wife — 'Black Vaughan' and 'Ellen the Terrible'. The lived at Hergest Court nearby, and their nicknames give some indication of their reputation. Ellen is reputed to have avenged the murder of her brother by dressing as a man, taking part in an archery tournament and killing the murderer with her first shot.

The old Grammar School is opposite the church. It was endowed in 1632 by Lady Margaret Hawkins, the wife of Admiral Sir John Hawkins, and built by John Abel. There are some attractive old cottages below the church on the other side, and down the road beyond them is the track of an early nineteenth-century horse tramway, part of a system that extended to Lyonshall, Eardisley and Hay.

It is fairly easy to explore the high ground around Kington on foot by following sections of the Offa's Dyke path. Rushock Hill is a worthwhile objective because the path goes by Bradnor Hill, a noted viewpoint. To reach the path you turn off Church Street at the Swan Inn, turn left into Common Close, and continue past the national school to a footbridge over the Back Brook. The path crosses the golf course, one of several claiming to be the highest in Britain, and after two miles or so reaches Rushock Hill, where there is a good surviving stretch of Dyke.

By taking the Dyke path in the opposite direction it is possible to get on to Hergest Ridge, which also provides magnificent views. Pass the church and take the turning to the left signposted 'Ridgebourne/Hergest Croft'. At the end of the lane is a gate giving access to the path, which can be followed all the way to Gladestry.

The name Hergest (pronounced 'Hargest', with a hard 'g') figures largely in this area. Hergest Croft, with its

Devils Mouth, Long Mynd

Ludlow Castle and town

Raglan Castle

famous gardens, is open to the public. It should not be confused with Hergest Court, which is not open but which is of great significance in Welsh cultural history. Nowadays it looks like a rather elaborate farmhouse, a mile from Kington on the Gladestry road, but it is immediately noticeable since it stands on high ground across a small valley. Two of the most famous collections of Welsh folk-tales, the Red and White Books of Hergest, were preserved here. The White Book was destroyed by fire in 1808, but the Red Book was translated from old to modern Welsh and then translated into English by Lady Charlotte Guest as *The Mabinogion* .

The route from Kington is the A4111 south to Eardisley. Since it is a long, straggling place, stretched out along the main road, it does not have the intimate atmosphere of some other Herefordshire villages; but some of its buildings deserve attention. The Tram Inn is a reminder of the railway from Kington mentioned earlier, and just around the corner from it is a small cruck cottage. The Forge in the main street is also of cruck construction. But one of the most attractive buildings is close to the church; it is a conversion of an old timber-framed barn into a terrace of four cottages, the sort of development that ought to be more common.

Also close to the church is the mound of a castle that was once extremely important — an unpopular thirteenth-century Bishop of Hereford was imprisoned here after a long record of extortion on behalf of Henry III and himself. The showpiece of the church is its remarkable Norman font, carved with the figures of a lion, two people fighting and a traditional 'harrowing of Hell'. Like so much of the church carving in Herefordshire, it conveys a sense of enjoyment in the craftsman rather than just a sense of duty, and scholars have been able to identify a definite style among these local craftsmen, who have come to be known as the Herefordshire School of Carving.

You turn on to the A4112 at Eardisley for the return to Leominster, but, if you have the time, there are various tempting diversions off the main road. At Almeley, for example, there is a particularly impressive manor house and a church with a sixteenth-century painted ceiling. At nearby Almeley Wooton is a Friends' Meeting House of 1672 which is of some importance in the history of the Society of Friends (the Quakers). An attraction of a different kind can be seen at Woonton, where a keen topiarist has transformed his front hedge in spectacular fashion.

The compulsory stop for anyone interested in architecture will be at Sarnesfield. Beside the church porch here is the tomb of John Abel, the master builder, who died in 1674 at the age of 97. He carved the tomb himself, including on it his wives as well as the tools of his trade. Many examples of his work have now been demolished, but the Grange at Leominster still stands, as does the old Grammar School at Kington and the roof and screen of Abbey Dore, described in the next chapter.

Soon after leaving Sarnesfield, on the right is the lofty spire of Weobley church. This small town has now been by-passed, and is a pleasant place for a leisurely stroll without intrusive traffic. On closer inspection, the spire is obviously something of a status symbol, being out of proportion to the rest of the church, and indeed Weobley was once one of the county's biggest and wealthiest boroughs, being specially noted for its ale. One of its most famous figures was Colonel John Birch, the

Parliamentary leader, who was MP for the town and settled here after the Restoration. His striking memorial is next to the altar in the church.

Weobley is rightly celebrated for being the architectural gem of the county, and it is impossible here to give a detailed account of it. The focal point, simply because the wide street suddenly narrows there, is the Red Lion, a fine building in itself but also hiding at its back a superb example of a cruck-framed house. The spacious air of the upper main street is partly the result of a fire which burned down an island of buildings in 1860 (they included John Abel's market hall), and a garden has now replaced them.

Not all the buildings are medieval, of course, and there are examples here of the widespread habit in the border counties of painting 'beams' on to whitened brick houses. Elsewhere in Britain this would be condemned as 'fakery', but here it can be seen as a mark of respect. The old Grammar School is one later structure (c 1660) which can compete with its older neighbours. If you are not overwhelmed by architecture after a walk round Weobley, it is worth the short journey south-west to the Ley (1589), one of the best timber-framed buildings in the county.

The by-pass has also brought tranquillity to the next village, Dilwyn, which once had a terrible traffic problem, with heavy lorries negotiating its tortuous main street. There is yet another fine church here, but the village has a unique feature invisible to all but the occasional pedestrian. At the point where the road from the village joins the by-pass on the Leominster side there is an underpass decorated with bright murals of the kind more often associated with trendy inner-city areas.

The parts of Herefordshire we have explored so far are associated with two rivers — the Lugg and the Arrow. The third and most famous is the Wye, and to reach it you turn south from Leominster and make for Hereford. This stretch of the A49 is of little interest except at Dinmore Hill, where the road climbs through woodland.

Hope-under-Dinsmore, at the bottom of the hill, is an example of a village thoughtlessly divided by road 'improvements' which have left the church and the school isolated from the village. The stately home to the east of Hope is Hampton Court, a house of great architectural interest as a rare example of a fortified fifteenth-century manor, built round a courtyard with a gatehouse. Built by Sir Roland Lenthall with money acquired during the Agincourt campaign, it was bought by the Earl and Countess of Coningsby, whose family later sold it to Richard Arkwright, son of the inventor. The Coningsbys' young son died in 1708 after choking on a cherry, and on a memorial in Hope church he is shown holding the fatal fruit. An ancestor founded the Coningsby Hospital in Hereford.

The house is, unfortunately, not open to the public, but part of the estate is. Richard Arkwright bought Dinmore Hill wood in 1810. Most of the original mature trees were felled during the First World War, and the area was reverting to scrub when it was acquired by the County Council in 1935. Since then an arboretum has been developed, and now it has become the 170-acre Queenswood Country Park, with a prominent entrance on the right of the road. There are specimens of over four hundred varieties of tree as well as a large area of oak woodland. A whole network of paths makes for pleasant walking, and

the Queen's View looks out over a
magnificent panorama from the
Malvern Hills to the Black Mountains.

Below Queenswood is Dinmore
Manor, which can be visited. Its most
interesting feature is the fourteenth-
century chapel of the Knights of St John
of Jerusalem. Other parts of the house
date from the seventeenth century, but
the sections open to the public are
mainly modern and of limited interest.
Before leaving Dinmore you should visit
Bodenham over to the east. It is a
'typically English' village, and untypical
of Herefordshire in that it is grouped
round a small village green, with a
church whose small spire sits oddly on
top of a large tower. In the spacious
interior there is a mysterious medieval
monument showing a woman and child.

After Dinmore the road drops
towards Hereford with the Lugg valley
on the left. Just before entering
Hereford, you cross the line of a Roman
road at Holmer, which has a church with
a detached tower and fine roof timbers.
The first problem in the city itself is
where to park the car; no stranger
should penetrate too far into its complex
road system. As you make for the city

The Old House, Hereford

centre you will see a turning to the left signposted 'Market Car Park'. You are strongly recommended to go there.

Most visitors to Hereford make straight for the Cathedral, but this is a mistake. Once there you are less likely to want to plunge back into the city to find out what you missed on the way. It is much better to make the Cathedral a peaceful end to your tour.

The Market Car Park is outside the town walls, which are delineated nowadays by a sort of grand prix racetrack known as a ring road. It is pleasant to see that Hereford banishes its fast traffic outside the walls, but it makes an approach to the city centre as hazardous as it must have been when the walls were defended. Before attempting the crossing you should walk back into Widemarsh Street to see the Coningsby Hospital and Blackfriars Gardens opposite Henley's Garage. As mentioned earlier, the Hospital was founded by a member of the Coningsby family of Hampton Court, near Dinsmore, in 1614, although the original buildings were of a much earlier date. The distinctive uniform of the pensioners here was supposed to have given a local girl, Nell Gwynne, the idea for the dress of Charles II's pensioners at the Royal Hospital, Chelsea. The building now houses tableaux and exhibits commemorating this aspect of its history, and there is also a small museum concerned with the Knights of St John of Jerusalem, whose hospice and chapel it had been. The Blackfriars Gardens are next door. They are all that remain of the monastery, but they contain a fourteenth-century preaching cross that is believed to be unique.

Widemarsh Street is the most direct route to the town centre. Once you are over the ring road you become aware of the homely timber-framed buildings and

small-scale architecture that characterises the city — a rather grandiose term for what is essentially a market town. You emerge at High Town, a pedestrianised area to the left, but if you turn right you will arrive after a few yards at the ancient church of All Saints, with its twisted spire. Apart from being a beautiful building in itself, it houses a chained library of three hundred books — the second largest in England (the largest is in the Cathedral). A presumptuous nineteenth-century churchwarden sold the lot to a dealer for £100, and the church authorities intervened just in time to prevent the sale.

Moving back to High Town, the lively hub of the city's shopping area, you will see at the far end a Jacobean house, looking oddly marooned like a ship in dry dock. This is the Old House, once part of a street called Butcher's Row and now preserved as a museum of seventeenth-century furniture and household effects.

The Old House is the last survivor of the buildings that once crowded this former market square. The greatest of all — reckoned to have been the finest timber-framed building in Europe — was the vast Guildhall, unthinkably demolished in 1862. On the evidence of old prints it was a breathtaking building. Red stones have been set into the paving of the precinct to mark the position of its piers.

Immediately behind the Old House is St Peter's, another of Hereford's medieval churches. Originally founded in 1074, it became a priory church in 1100 and a parish church in 1131, its demotion being due to the completion of the Cathedral. The building in classical style on the other side of St Peter's Square is the Shire Hall, designed by Robert Smirke in the early nineteenth century.

St Owen's Street leads away from St Peter's Square, and contains some distinguished Georgian architecture; it is also a convenient route to the site of the castle, which is reached by turning right into St Ethelbert Street. Castle Green stands high above the river. There are no remains of the castle itself apart from nearby Castle Cliffe, a building that has had many uses. It was the Governor's house during the Civil War, became the county gaol, was converted into a private house in 1796, and now houses a canoe training centre. The monument in the middle of Castle Green, incidentally, is the local Nelson's Column, erected in 1809.

From Castle Green it is possible to cross the river by the Victoria footbridge and admire the view of the Cathedral as you walk through Bishop's Meadow to the Old Wye Bridge, which dates from 1100. It is difficult now to believe that this bridge carried all traffic in and out of the city until 1967. On the other side, the first turning on the right takes you into Gwynne Street, where a plaque marks Nell's birthplace, and, if you continue through Palace Yard, you confront Broad Street, Hereford's most impressive thoroughfare.

The eye-catching building here is the splendid Green Dragon Hotel, and below it on the left is the city library and museum, well worth visiting for a wide variety of exhibits covering many spheres of interest. Other notable buildings here include the former town house of the Duke of Norfolk opposite the hotel and, at the bottom on the right, St Xavier's Roman Catholic Church. All Saints church and spire closes off the end of the street as you look up it.

Now to the Cathedral. Tradition claims that Hereford has had a bishop since the seventh century (although he probably had a roving commission and was not resident) and it is likely that the first Cathedral was erected in about 730. Nothing remains of this building or of anything before the Norman Conquest; the present Cathedral seems to have been started in 1080 and has been added to ever since. The whole structure is now beautifully maintained, but it was not always so. On Easter Monday 1786 there was a catastrophe when the west tower fell, destroying part of the nave. In his book 'The River Wye' Keith Kissack gives an entertaining account of this and other near-disasters, quoting the Hereford Journal's casual comment that 'the ruins, though awful, afford a pleasing view, especially to behold the statues of kings and bishops resting one upon the other'.

The next fifty years saw half-hearted and muddled attempts at restoration, done as cheaply as possible and in poor taste. It was during this period that the Cathedral came close to losing its priceless chained library of over 1400 books — in 1842 they were stored in a lumber room, and the Dean of the time warned that unless they were shifted the 'rubbish' would be burnt! The library is now in the north choir aisle and is open to visitors for a short period each weekday; it includes some superb illuminated works and many thousands of early medieval manuscripts. Another treasure is the 700-year-old Map of the World, drawn by Richard de Bello in the late thirteenth century. The map shows the Garden of Eden, Noah's Ark, Lot's Wife, the Sphinx and the Pillars of Hercules as well as more factual information.

The shrine of St Thomas of Hereford in the north transept is a reminder of the last of the pre-Reformation English saints. Thomas de Cantilupe was Bishop here from 1274 to 1282, and after he had

City Museum and Art Gallery, Broad Street
Archaeology and natural history of Herefordshire; also costumes, toys, textiles, militaria, folk history.

Regimental Museum, 1st Battalion, Herefordshire Light Infantry, Harold Street
Open only by appointment. (see Further Information)

Coningsby Chapel and Museum, Widemarsh Street
Formerly the Hospice and Chapel of the Knights of St John of Jerusalem. Exhibits relating to the Order displayed in Chapel. On 1st floor a series of tableaux illustrating the life of the Coningsby Pensioners.

Herefordshire Waterworks Museum, Broomy Hill
Reconstructed Victorian waterworks, collection of pumping engines and other similar industrial and transport exhibits.

Museum of Cider, Rylands Street
History of traditional cider-making. Reconstructed farm cider-house, cooper's shop, 1920s cider factory etc.

Bulmer Railway Centre, Whitecross Road
GWR steam loco 'King George V', with variety of rolling stock including royal coach. Occasional steam days.

The Old House, High Town
Jacobean House furnished in seventeenth century style.

Churchill Gardens Museum, Venn's Lane
Extensive costume collection, furniture, glass, procelain, paintings.

Cathedral
Chained library of over 1400 books, Mappa Mundi, Early English Lady Chapel and much else of interest.

All Saints Church
Chained library, open by arrangement (information at church).

City Walls
Remains visible in Victoria Street and West Street.

Parks and Sports Facilities, Park at Castle Green, east of Cathedral Bishop's Meadow and King George VI Playing Fields, riverside opposite Cathedral. Tennis, putting, paddling pool, indoor swimming pool, boating.

Theatre and Cinema, Nell Gwynne Theatre, Edgar Street
Amateur and professional productions. Focus Cinema, High Town.

Markets, Newmarket Street
Livestock market on Wednesdays. General market Wednesdays and Saturdays.

died in Italy his bones were brought back to Hereford. After hundreds of reports of miracles at his tomb, he was canonised in 1307.   The Cathedral authorities have made various concessions to the demands of tourists, including refreshments in the Chapter House yard and a discreetly-screened area in the south-east corner of the Cathedral where books and postcards are on sale. In the peak tourist season, however, it is nice to see that every visitor is welcomed and given a leaflet drawing attention to the historic and contemporary purposes of the building.

Between the Cathedral and the river are two further places of interest. The detached Bishop's Palace has a bland Victorian air, concealing the fact that it may well be the oldest domestic timber-framed building in England, with a hall dating from the late twelfth century. At the south-east end of the Cathedral are the fifteenth-century former lodgings of the minor orders among the staff — the College of Vicars Choral.

You can return to Widemarsh Street and the car by walking up the pleasant shopping lane called Church Street, which leads away from the north front of the Cathedral. You will not have exhausted Hereford's attractions, however. There is a whole riverside area, recalling that the city was once a thriving river port and shipbuilding town. It is described in an interesting pamphlet called *A Walk in Hereford along the River Wye*, produced by the Hereford Civic Trust. Another of the Trust's publications, *The Principal Walk in Hereford* is a detailed commentary guide to the main features of interest in the town centre.

There is some attractive countryside west of Hereford, much of it dominated by the river Wye. The Brecon road brings you after about four miles to King's Acre, where you branch right on to the A480. Credenhill is remembered because of its associations with the poet Thomas Traherne, who became Rector here in 1652 after starting life in Hereford as the son of a shoemaker. Oddly enough, the son of another Rector of Credenhill also made history

in a way — H P Bulmer started making cider here before moving his business into Hereford in 1887. The village itself is unremarkable, but the church has some good fourteenth-century stained glass.

The church is also the showpiece of Brinsop, containing as it does some of the finest work of the Herefordshire School of Carvers, as well as a fourteenth-century rood screen and some fine glass. The memorials in the church indicate that the local squires were the Daunseys of Brinsop Court. Wordsworth frequently stayed here when visiting his wife's brother, and it would be interesting to know what he made of this moated manor-house, 600 years old and looking well today. Mansell Lacy is tucked away off the main road; most tourists stop only long enough to photograph the half-timbered post office with its dove-cot, but it is worth lingering to admire the buildings of what seems an enviable place in which to live.

You now move into an area covered earlier in the chapter, and it is best to turn left on to the minor road at Calver Hill and make for the A438 again. But before turning back towards Hereford along the Wye valley, you should carry on as far as Rhydspence, which is not really a village but an inn. You can hardly miss it, as it stands in a commanding position by the road. Dating from the sixteenth century, it was once known simply as the Cattle Inn because it was an important staging post for drovers as they brought their beasts from Wales to the English markets. There were shoeing facilities here for the oxen, but equally important were the drinking facilities, and Kilvert notes in his diary that noise and singing often went on well into the night.

At the bottom of the hill below

Rhydspence is a turning for Brilley. It is a long climb through a scattered village with some interesting early houses, but as you level out at the top there is a tiny National Trust signpost marked Cwmmau Farmhouse. The narrow road leads down to an area of common with views over the Wye, and a little way beyond is the farmhouse itself. It has been preserved by the Trust as an example of a traditional Herefordshire Farmhouse, with timber-framing and stone roof-cladding. Unfortunately, it is open freely to the public only at Easter and on certain bank holidays, although a private visit can be arranged in advance by writing to the occupier. It is worth taking the trouble because so much of the county's architecture can only be admired from the outside; at Cwmmau the building techniques can be studied in detail.

There is now a choice of routes to Hereford on either side of the river, and the lack of bridges makes it difficult to move from one to the other. Perhaps the best compromise is to take the A438 to Letton and then turn right for Bredwardine, where Francis Kilvert ended his days. He was 39 when he died from peritonitis a few weeks after his marriage in 1879. His tomb is in the churchyard.

Bredwardine itself is a pleasant village with a church containing several Norman features, an attractive inn and the remains of a castle next to the church. Its fine six-arched bridge is one of the few along this stretch of the river to have survived frequent severe floods in the past. There is a chance here to walk up above Bredwardine and see Arthur's Stone, an ancient burial chamber. At the crossroads by the Red Lion take the Moccas road, then the first turning to the right towards Dorstone. Turn right after about a mile on to a lane which passes the Stone. As you face south here, you are at the head of the Golden Valley, described in the next chapter. Continue down on the same lane, turning right at the junction.

Moccas Court, a little way along the river, is open to the public. It is a classic eighteenth-century house and very elegant indeed, with a beautiful circular drawing room decorated unusually with French paper panels. Definitely a place for the connoisseur.

It is a good idea to stay on this side of the river in order to visit the church at Madley, which is noted for its unusual size and splendour (the font is said to be the second largest in England). It was a considerable place of pilgrimage in the fourteenth century, and most of it dates from that time. The east window has some medieval stained glass, although this is outshone by the glass at Eaton Bishop, four miles away.

There is an opportunity for a gentle riverside walk at Eaton Bishop. Follow the main road north of the church and turn right after half a mile at Lane Head Farm. The lane and path take you down to the Wye, where there is a path to the right along the bank. Pass over a footbridge into a field and join a track which brings you out on to a road close to the Camp Inn. Turn right here and then left at the telephone kiosk past some fine houses. Turn right at the junction near the small bridge and left at the next one, to re-enter the village.

The return to Hereford is over the new Wye Bridge, which is the starting point for the next chapter of this guide.

7 Abergavenny, Hay and the Black Mountains

The southernmost area of the border country includes the Black Mountains and their associated valleys. In many ways, it is a romantic countryside of isolated small towns and remote villages, and in the past it has nurtured or attracted some romantic figures. The great central mass of hills dictates the boundaries of the area and give it unity; the Welsh border divides it on the map

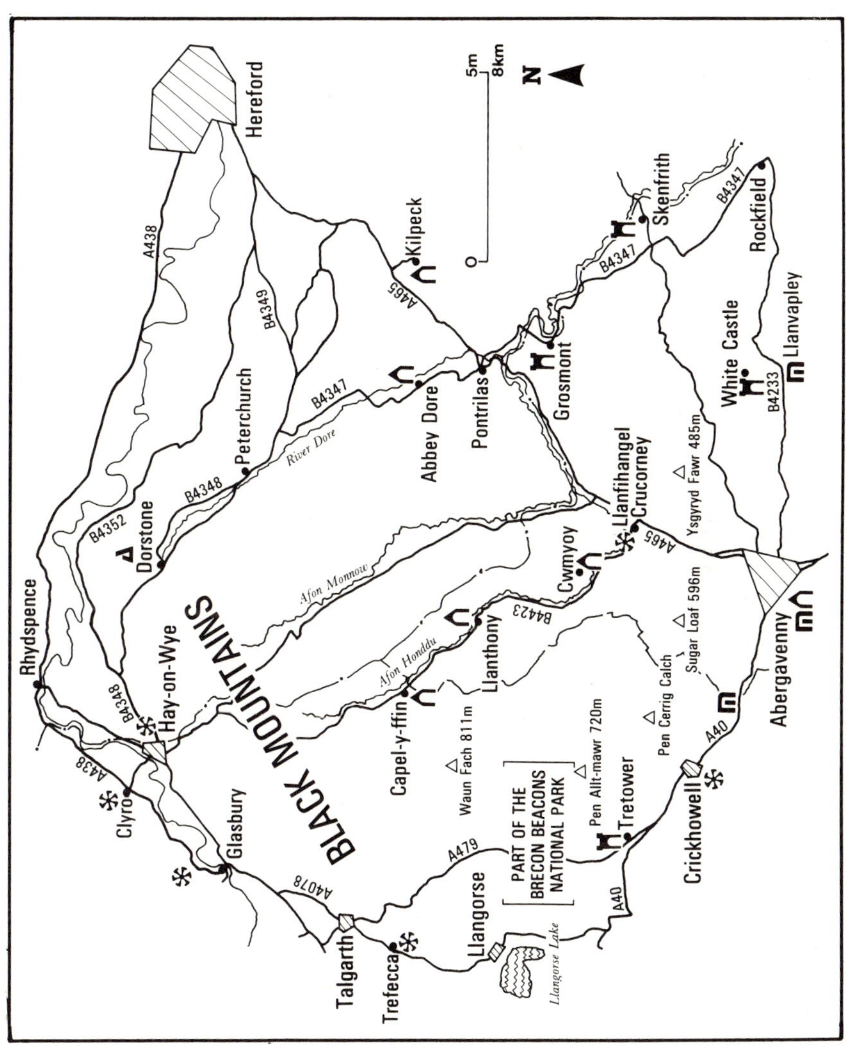

but has never had much practical significance.

This point is illustrated very soon after you leave Hereford on the A465, because almost at once you enter a part of Herefordshire full of Welsh placenames. This is the territory known in post-Norman times as Archenfield. For 200 years after the Conquest, it remained a pocket of Welshness in an otherwise English environment. The inhabitants had a reputation for extreme loyalty to the English crown — in fact they had the 'privilege' of forming the vanguard of the English armies in their campaigns against the Welsh. In return the people were allowed to observe Welsh law and customs.

Needless to say, they were regarded as traitors by other Welshmen, who extracted revenge whenever possible. Even today, the area has a distinctive atmosphere of 'no-man's-land', consisting of scattered farms and tiny hamlets, with churches often isolated from settlements. The first feature of interest is off the road to the left about a mile after the village of Didley (signposted 'Kilpeck'). You pass the solitary church of St Devereux to reach Kilpeck, which is an attractive mixture of stone and timber-frame houses. What attracts thousands of visitors (and many scholars) each year is the small sandstone church, which many believe to be the most remarkable in Britain.

It has a profusion of carving, the work of the anonymous men who formed what has come to be known as the Herefordshire School of Carving. Their work is widespread throughout the county, but at Kilpeck they excelled themselves, producing a riot of decoration in many moods — moral, religious, historical and frivolous. Every aspect of medieval life is depicted here, both inside and outside the church.

It is a Norman building, and one that survived Victorian restoration very well — the nineteenth century certainly did not share the medieval belief that all aspects of human life were fit subjects for church decoration. Other features to note are the enormous font and the tub-like stoup with carved hands clasped round it.

From Kilpeck it is possible to reach Pontrilas without returning to the main road. You cannot miss it because it is dominated by vast sawmills. The right turn on to the B4347 is the way into the Golden Valley, a name which has a disappointingly prosaic origin — at some point the Welsh 'dwr' (water) became confused with 'd'or' (golden). The valley is over twelve miles long and forms the course of the river Dore, which rises above Hay-on-Wye.

The first village encountered, Ewyas Harold, is not exactly beautiful or impressive, although at the time of the Doomsday Book it was one of only five boroughs in the county, and there are records of merchants from France visiting its fairs in the fourteenth century. Nowadays it has a modern, functional appearance, and the only reminder of its former importance is the castle mound. The recently-built Roman Catholic church is in some ways more interesting than the parish church, although the latter has a memorial that has puzzled people for a long time. It is of fourteenth century origin and shows a woman holding a heart in her hands.

The famous Dore Abbey is a few minutes' drive up the valley road, but it is also possible to walk there over the Common. You start in the lane at the back of the church, turn left at the junction and follow the lane round and over a cattle grid. Keep to the left-hand track, which brings you out on to a lane west of the Abbey.

The big church is all that remains of the Cistercian Abbey, but it is impressive nevertheless, mainly because you do not expect to see such a large building standing in very ordinary fields. When Henry VIII dissolved the great monastic houses, Abbey Dore came into the hands of the Scudamore family, and the first Viscount commissioned John Abel to restore it from its ruinous condition. In the process, over 200 tons of oak were used in the roof, and the twelfth-century altar was retrieved from a farmyard. It was re-consecrated in 1634. One of its outstanding features is the substantial and elaborate chancel screen carved by Abel himself.

It is worth turning left after Abbey Dore to visit the churches at Bacton and St Margaret's. There is nothing remarkable about Bacton church itself, but it is noted for an effigy of Blanche Parry, lady-in-waiting to Elizabeth I. She took on her duties when the future Queen was only three years old and remained in royal service for the rest of her life. It condemned her, of course, to spinsterhood, a fact which is much praised in the accompanying inscription. It is said that one of the church's treasures — an elaborately-embroidered altar frontal — is Blanche Parry's work.

You reach St Margaret's by climbing steeply out of Bacton and following signposts until you see directions to the Sun Inn. This stands just below the church and seems equally isolated. From the outside the church looks unpromisingly plain, standing in a roughly-mown field. It is an exposed spot, commanding wide views, but it was precisely this remoteness that saved the magnificent rood screen from destruction after the Reformation. Recent work has been done on the original wall texts, and they are now

Dore Abbey

bright and clean with their former
lettering. The one over the door as you
leave says dauntingly 'Go and sin no
more'. The intricate screen conceals the
Norman chancel arch, to one side of
which is a stone staircase leading to the
rood loft. The church richly repays the
tortuous drive.

Soon after returning to the main road
you cross the river and also the track of
the old railway that once linked Hay
with the Hereford-Abergavenny line.

At Vowchurch you have the odd
prospect of two churches facing each
other across the river and separated by a
few hundred yards. The one on the
opposite bank belongs to the tiny hamlet
of Turnastone. Vowchurch's own parish
church is unusual for having its roof
supported on wooden posts set in the
walls. Poston camp, to the north-west, is
one of the few hill forts in the border
country to have been systematically
investigated, and the finds have included
some rare first-century native pottery.
To the east is Monnington Court, built
near the site of a house once occupied by
the Scudamore family in which Owain
Glyndwr took refuge with his daughter-
in-law just before his death.

Peterchurch is the unofficial 'capital'
of the valley in that it has a secondary
school and also the finest parish church.
The spire is plastic — the original
fourteenth-century one was taken down
some years ago — but the rest is genuine
and rather unusual inside; three arches
of decreasing height divide the church
down its length. Another interesting
feature is the memorial on the wall
showing a carp with a chain round its
neck, alleged to commemorate the
catching of a fish in St Peter's Well
nearby.

Wellbrook Manor, a short distance
east of the church, is a famous example
of a hall-house of the fourteenth

century. The stone exterior is timber-
framed inside, and part of the house is of
cruck construction.

Dorstone lies at the head of the valley,
one of the many border settlements
which failed to develop into boroughs. It
has the characteristic sequence of castle,
market-place and church, although only
the motte and bailey remain of the
castle, and the church was largely rebuilt
in 1889. Richard de Brito, one of the
knights who murdered Thomas aì
Becket, came here after completing a

PLACES OF INTEREST SOUTH OF
HEREFORD

Kilpeck Church, off A465, 8m south-
west of Hereford
Famous medieval carving, inside and
out, and other features of interest.

Dore Abbey, off A465 in Golden
Valley
Surviving church of Cistercian abbey.
Fine roof work and carved screen.

St Margaret's Church, 4m north-west
of Dore Abbey
Remote church with superb rood
screen and unusual wall texts.

Arthur's Stone
Neolithic burial chamber above
Dorstone, at head of Golden Valley.

Grosmont church, off A465, 3m south
of Pontrilas
Unusual church with rare example of
'abandoned' nave.

The 'Trilateral' castles
Group of three castles — Grosmont,
Skenfrith, White Castle —
surrounding Graig Syfyrddin.

period of penance in Palestine. He founded a chapel in the church in 1256, as recorded on a stone found during the rebuilding.

Another building of interest in Dorstone is the school on the south side of the market place, founded in 1643 to provide a free education for the village children. The site of the original terminus of the Golden Valley railway can still be traced on the edge of the village by the river bridge. It was opened in 1881, but was wildly unprofitable, even after it had been extended to Hay in 1889. The passenger service ceased in 1941 and the line was closed altogether in 1957.

Dorstone is best known for the burial chamber known as Arthur's Stone, which can be reached by a track leading off the main road at GR 318422. The connection with Arthur is dubious, but the tomb, with its huge capstone, is a remarkable structure, estimated as being of Neolithic origin. Until the mid-nineteenth century, it was the gathering-place for village celebrations.

The return to Pontrilas can be made either on the same road or by a series of rather more interesting minor roads over the hills to the west. If you decide on the latter you should leave Dorstone on the Snodhill road. Snodhill, about a mile to the south, is famous because of an entertaining description in Kilvert's diary of a typically elaborate Victorian picnic on its castle site. This extends to about ten acres with some substantial remains, and is still a good place for a picnic. One of the features of the village is the number of farmsteads with the local sandstone roof cladding.

You go south from Snodhill on a narrow road that rises and falls steeply in places. Standing isolated at the side of the road at GR 310379 is the Urishay chapel, probably Norman in origin, with the site of Urishay castle next to it. The remains of a large seventeenth-century house now stand on the motte. There are fine views from here, but it remains a rather desolate spot.

An OS map is needed now to negotiate the tangle of narrow lanes. When you reach the junction at GR 317365 you should continue south to the next crossroads and then turn right to reach the hamlet of Michaelchurch Escley. It is worth visiting the church to see the large wall painting — a traditional representation of Christ of the Trades, showing Christ surrounded by an assortment of tools.

You now follow the lonely road that runs by the Escley Brook down to Longtown. The main village is on another road over to the right, and the fact that there is a mountain rescue post is a reminder that just to the west are some of the most formidable areas of the Black Mountains. There are two castles at Longtown. One, simply a motte and bailey, is situated out of the village to the south, where the Olchon Brook joins the river Monnow. The other is at the northern end and has some interesting ruins.

There are two readily-accessible hill walks from Longtown. The first is along the ridge to the Red Daren, and can be reached by taking the lane leading out of the village at GR 326286. (For those willing to negotiate rather hazardous lanes in the car there is a car park and picnic site just below the Red Daren, reached by leaving Longtown by the road to the north and turning left on to a signposted road after a mile.)

The start of the second walk is reached by travelling two miles to Llanveynoe. The church here is interesting because of the two memorial stones (probably tenth century) set in its south wall. In the churchyard is a Celtic

Cross, possibly of the same age. The track beginning at GR 303315 will take you straight to Little Black Hill and then on to the rocky ridge of the Black Hill itself (known locally as the Cat's Back). Once again, it is possible to make a nearer approach in the car by continuing past Llanveynoe church for a mile, branching right and then right again where the picnic area is signposted. From Black Hill you can walk the five miles north to Hay Bluff if you wish.

Moving south from Longtown, you very quickly reach Clodock. The church here was founded, according to legend, when Clydawg, King of Ewyas, was murdered on a hunting expedition in 540. The oxen drawing the cart with his body on it refused to cross the ford here, so the King was buried nearby. The church was built on the spot and dedicated to him. It is a fascinating building with some seventeenth-century box pews, a three-decker pulpit, a musicians' gallery and a rare example of a three-sided communion rail.

Make sure you take the road on the west of the river when you leave Clodock — the route on the other side is complicated, to say the least. You emerge on to the A465 at Pandy after a tour that has taken in some of the wildest Herefordshire countryside. The river Monnow, which now takes in the river Honddu, curves away east and goes on to achieve a respectable size as it flows through Monmouth and Chepstow to the Severn estuary.

It is worth pointing out here that one of the highest and loneliest stretches of the Offa's Dyke path starts at Pandy and continues along the ridges of the Black Mountains to Hay. It is a potentially dangerous walk, definitely for the experienced only, and the usual precautions should be taken before starting on it. You reach it by a turning opposite the Lancaster Arms in Pandy.

The countryside to the south of the Golden Valley is not so exciting scenically, but it contains much of interest. Pontrilas is again the starting point. Take the B4347 down the Monnow valley for Grosmont, which has one of the 'Tri-lateral' castles — a group of three situated around Graig Syfyrddu, the others being Skenfrith and White Castle. Grosmont village is a comfortable, lived-in place with a market hall that seems to have been recently restored. The church and the castle stand on opposite sides of the main street.

One is surprised, on entering the church, to step into what appears at first to be a dim lumber-room with a rough floor and two rows of arches. In one corner is a grotesque, shapeless effigy, together with (at the time of writing) a horse plough, an antique farm cart and something resembling an old mangle. This is, in fact, the nave of the church. The building was originally of a size designed to indicate the importance of Grosmont. Unfortunately it was always too big for the congregation, and as the numbers of worshippers declined further, only the chancel was used for services. When the church was restored in 1870, a glazed screen was put up to shut off the nave entirely, and now the contrast between the rough austerity of the nave and the richness of the chancel is startling.

The castle is impressively situated on a rounded hill above a deep moat. It has a keep, a gatehouse and high curtain walls, but the most unusual feature is the delicate fourteenth-century chimney, a relic of the banqueting hall.

Continuing down the road with Garway Hill on the left, you arrive at Skenfrith Castle after about three miles. Skenfrith, now an attractive village, was

Grosmont Castle

one of many places in the border which started promisingly as settlements but failed to survive; in this case, it was due to the increasing prominence of its neighbour Grosmont, which acquired the vital market. The castle is the least impressive of the three and was never of major military importance, although John of Gaunt was once Governor. It has an extensive round keep within a bailey with towers at each corner. The sandstone church has a heavily-buttressed tower and a fine 'double-decker' belfry, and the interior is of interest, with memorials to the Morgan family. Their seventeenth-century pew can still be seen. The church's main treasure, however, is an embroidered fifteenth-century cope.

Three miles to the south is Rockfield, the estate village of Rockfield House. This is the home of the Rolls family, whose best-known member was the Hon. Charles, co-founder of Rolls-Royce. You turn right here on to the Abergavenny road and follow it to Llantilio Crossenny, where a right turn leads up to White Castle. The name is a reminder that these castles looked a little different in the middle ages when they were coated with primitive paint or plaster and must have gleamed in the sun. It is the best-preserved of the Trilateral castles, though unlike the other two it has no accompanying settlement. The remains include inner and outer wards, a towered gatehouse and moats.

The hill to the west of White Castle, dominating the whole landscape is Ysgyryd Fawr (or Skirrid). It is National Trust property, and the best way to reach the top is to continue north from White Castle, turn left on to the B4521 and follow it to a point about two miles from Abergavenny when you are right under the hill. There is a lay-by on the right, and a little further on a National Park boundary sign by a stile. The walk is waymarked from here and proceeds through a plantation to the southern end of the hill, where a path continues to the summit at 1596ft.

Skirrid is a hill of great religious significance. To the west of the summit is a huge cleft, caused, according to legend, by the hill splitting when the veil of the temple was rent at the Crucifixion. The trigonometrical point at the top stands in the still-traceable ruins of a chapel dedicated to St Michael, which received papal approval as an object of pilgrimage.

It is time now to explore the second and most dramatic of the Black Mountain valleys — the Vale of Ewyas. Access is via Llanfihangel Crucorny on the A465, where the B4423 turns into the Vale. A word of warning: this road starts as a broad highway but very soon narrows, and in the holiday season it can be notoriously congested. At some points it is single-lane only, and the blind corners are certain to banish any enjoyment on the driver's part. One reason for the traffic is that the road becomes a scenic drive to Hay at the northern end of the Vale. Only two solutions are possible — come very early or very late, or walk.

The Offa's Dyke path on the ridge to the right is certainly the most relaxed way to see the Vale, since the walker can branch off from it to see the two main attractions — Llanthony Priory and Capel-y-Ffin. A careful study of the OS map will reveal possible paths on the east side of the river Honddu at least as far as the Priory.

However you decide to tackle the Vale, Llanfihangel Crucorny is worth stopping to see. The Skirrid Inn is supposedly Norman in origin, but its present structure is medieval. Its most interesting feature is its oak staircase (you will have to ask permission to see it), where sheep-stealers were apparently lynched when the building was a courthouse. On Sunday afternoons in summer it is possible to visit Llanfihangel Court, the entrance to which is opposite the church. The gardens of this Tudor mansion are famous for their tree-lined avenues and for their fine views of the Skirrid.

This is an area of curious and highly individual churches, and there could be no better example than the church at Cwmyoy, about two miles further up the valley. It stands in an isolated position on the east side of the river, and there are two approach roads; you are strongly advised to take the second turning through Neuadd farm, leave the car at the first opportunity and then walk. There is hardly any parking space at the church itself.

It has been in the past the victim of landslip, with the result that its tower and walls lean in all directions, supported by heavy buttresses. The effect is even more alarming inside, where there is hardly a perpendicular wall. If one disregards all this, the interior is superb. The tiny chancel and sanctuary are at a much higher level than the nave; combined with the effect of the low roof, this gives the east end a peculiarly intimate atmosphere. Look at the churchyard, too. The gravestones are fine examples of the local stonemason's art, and there is a moving memorial to

The 'leaning' church at Cwmyoy

Jane Thomas and her baby at the south-east corner of the church, close to the old churchyard cross. The hummocks of the landslip are still very much in evidence above the church.

A fine walk can be started at Cwmyoy. Take the path due north of the church and go north-west to the farm at Daren. From here the path continues along the lower slopes to Maesyberan, where you climb sharply up to the Offa's Dyke path on the ridge. The way back is along the top of Hatterall Hill.

As you return to the valley road and drive towards Llanthony, the rocky outcrops above Cwmyoy and the bleak summits on both sides of the road leave no doubt as to why a religious order seeking total seclusion should have selected Llanthony as the site for a priory. Until fairly recently, access to the further reaches of this valley were difficult and often impossible in winter, and not very easy in a wet summer.

Be careful not to miss the entrance to the priory; there is no parking elsewhere, and once you are past you will probably not be able to turn round. A group of Augustinian monks formed a community here at the beginning of the twelfth century, but it was not long before local warfare between the Welsh and the Normans drove them away in search of security. They established a new home, called Llanthony Secunda, near Gloucester, and although a fresh start was made in the Vale of Ewyas in about 1175 there was continual rivalry between the old and new establishments. The two became independent in 1205,

Abergavenny Museum
In shooting lodge in castle grounds.
Local history, rural crafts,
reconstruction of Welsh border
kitchen etc.

Priory church
Noted for its size and the number of
its memorials. Open only at limited
times (see notice in porch). Tithe
barn next door.

Leisure Centre, Old Hereford Road
Swimming pool, squash, sports hall
etc. Available to public out of school
hours and during school holidays.
Tel: 2701.

Partrishow church, 6m north of
Abergavenny at GR 279225
Remote church with magnificent
rood screen and other interesting
features.

Rural Crafts Museum, Llanvapley,
4m east of Abergavenny on B4233
Agricultural exhibits and all aspects
of rural life.

The Welsh Gallery, 18 Cross Street
Exhibitions by Welsh artists and
craftsmen.

In the Vale of Ewyas:
Cwmyoy church, $2\frac{1}{2}$ miles north west
of Llanfihangel Crucorny
Famous 'leaning' church, victim of
landslip.

Llanthony Priory
Remains of 11th/12th century Priory
church. Also parish church in former
infirmary.

Capel-y-Ffin
Remains of Llanthony 'Abbey',
founded by 'Father Ignatius', who is
buried there. Also interesting small
Anglican and Baptist chapels.

---

but it was the Gloucester community
which flourished; in 1481 it received
royal authority to take over the older
priory, which was by now almost
deserted.

When both communities were
dissolved in 1538, Llanthony fell into
private hands and little was done to
maintain it. A shooting lodge was built
into the ruins at the beginning of the
nineteenth century, and in 1807 the
whole place was bought by the poet
Walter Savage Landor, who had
ambitious plans to develop the estate.
Living temporarily in the shooting
lodge, he started to build a house above
the ruins, but intense local hostility and
a stream of litigation forced him to
leave, virtually bankrupt, in 1815. A
special fund was set up to pay for the
restoration of the ruins, but it was not
until the 1930s that systematic work
began.

In recent years the shooting lodge has
become a small hotel, but the remaining
ruins can be visited, preferably out of
season or late in the evening, when
something of the atmosphere that
attracted the original settlers can still be
sensed. The ruins mainly comprise the
two magnificent towers of the west end,
a centre tower and the north nave
arcade. The gatehouse, now used as a
barn, stands apart from the main site
close to the road.

The long, low building that was
probably once the infirmary is now the
parish church of St David. The plain

interior is relieved by a remarkable group of slate memorial tablets on each side of the chancel, and it is pleasant to see the old oil lamps still in position.

3½
**

A short walk above the priory is waymarked. It passes some of the woodland planted by Landor and also the remains of his ill-fated house. The start of the walk is the field at the back of the ruins.

6½
**

Opposite the lane to the priory there is access to a footbridge over the river, and from here you can start a walk to the summit of Bal Mawr on the western side of the valley. Keep to the right after the bridge and ascend Cwm Bwchel on the right hand side. Once at the top, Bal Mawr can be approached virtually direct; at 2000ft it provides exceptional views. To return, go due south to the edge of the plantation and pick up the path at GR 270263, which takes you back down to the valley via Henllan. To avoid getting entangled with traffic, take the track which passes through the length of the plantation just above the road and passes Sunnybank at GR 289270, bringing you back to the footbridge.

After Llanthony the valley road becomes officially 'minor' and even more trying during the holiday season. Luckily, it is possible to come here very early or very late in the day because there are no official hours of opening at Capel-y-Ffin, four miles further up the valley. The tiny hamlet —'The Chapel on the Boundary' — was the scene of a remarkable episode at the end of the nineteenth century.

The Revd Joseph Leycester Lyne, born in 1837 and ordained deacon in the Anglican Church in 1860, became a famous figure of the Anglo-Catholic revival, calling himself Father Ignatius and claiming to have been called to re-establish English monasticism. He attempted to acquire Llanthony Priory for this purpose, but having failed he decided to build a monastery from scratch at Capel-y-Ffin, calling his community Llanthony Tertia.

By means of a series of preaching tours he raised enough money to start building in 1870. His charismatic personality was sufficient to attract recruits, and the establishment survived rather precariously until 1908, when he died. His successors failed to achieve the drive and fund-raising successes of the founder, and the community eventually linked itself with a monastery on the island of Caldy, whose members entered the Roman Catholic Church in 1913.

Opinions differed sharply on the subject of Father Ignatius, but there is little doubt that he was a sincere and idealistic man who failed to see that his unorthodox methods could be misunderstood, both locally and further afield. All that now remains of the monastery church is the roofless nave and chancel containing the grave slab of Father Ignatius, maintained by a Memorial Trust set up in 1968.

The residential quarters, privately owned, are nearby. They were bought in 1924 by the sculptor and designer Eric Gill with the aim of setting up another community, this time of artists. This venture also failed, mainly because of the poor communications in the valley.

To visit the monastery church, take the minor road to the left in Capel-y-Ffin for a few hundred yards and cross the stile set into a stone archway on the left. The path up to the buildings is short but very steep. There is no access to the other buildings unless you intend to go pony-trekking.

Do not miss the little eighteenth-century church in Capel-y-Ffin with its odd leaning belfry. It may well be the smallest you will ever see, but even so it has a miniature west gallery and shows every sign of being well cared-for. The Baptist chapel, very similar in style, is beyond it on the other side of the stream.

You can walk up to the Gospel Pass from here by a route that is fairly severe and exposed in places. Continue along the lane past the monastery for a mile and cross the stream, after which a track heads north-west past Blaen Bwch. It then becomes a path which follows the stream and eventually reaches the Twmpa at 2200ft (you reach the ridge at GR 220347). Follow the ridge down to the road at GR 236353 and return to Capel-y-Ffin. It is worth pointing out that on the way back you pass one of the country's more inaccessible Youth Hostels at The Castle.

The road north of Capel-y-Ffin winds its way to a cattle grid and then suddenly emerges on to magnificent open mountainside, providing at long last a chance to park and look at the view back down the valley. You then drive across broad expanses of upland and start the descent towards Hay. When you see the panorama in front of you the congestion on the road is explained. Hay is described later in the chapter; for the moment we return to the bottom of the valley and into Abergavenny.

As you approach the town from the east you are struck at once by the hills that surround it. Immediately ahead is the looming Blorenge, and it is hard to believe that on the other side of it are the industrial valleys of South Wales. Equally prominent on the right is the Sugar Loaf, and between them lies the Usk Valley. A glance at the map shows that the valley is a strategic route into central Wales, and Abergavenny, at its head, has always been of historical importance. The Romans had a fortress here called Gobanium, a motte and bailey was built around 1100, and a more substantial castle was erected in the twelfth century.

In summer, Abergavenny has the

Abergavenny castle with the 'Sugar Loaf' in the background

bustling air of a tourist centre, but out of season it becomes the sort of border town with which we are now familiar — grey, rather drab, not caring too much about appearances and generally carrying out the unromantic but necessary functions of a rural centre. Even so, it has an honourable place in Welsh cultural history because it was here that the Welsh Literary Society was founded in 1833, meeting at the Sun Inn. The annual Eisteddfod, held for 21 years, was a vital factor in encouraging the revival of the Welsh language.

The main street is dominated at its top end by the huge Town Hall and Market, complete with clock tower, a grandiose Victorian complex that fits uneasily into the small-scale architecture of the town. The gem of the street is undoubtedly the Angel Hotel, early nineteenth-century, but looking older. The castle is at the

bottom end, and what remains of it has a very placid air, since the grounds have been tidied up to the point where neatness has taken away any impressiveness the site may once have had. What appears to be a keep in a remarkable state of preservation, is in fact, an early-Victorian shooting lodge, now in service as the town museum.

The Priory Church of St Mary is all that survives of the great Benedictine Priory established by Hamelin de Ballon soon after the Conquest. It is a cathedral-like building, remarkable for the large number of memorials, mainly commemorating the families of Marcher lords, but its outstanding feature is an immense effigy of Jesse, father of David, carved from a single piece of oak and possibly of fourteenth-century origin. The medieval choir stalls are also worthy of note. Unfortunately, the church is normally kept locked on most weekdays, and if you wish to see the interior you will need to contact the local information centre in advance to discover the current arrangements.

At the side of the church the cavernous tithe barn still stands, used now as commercial premises. The town has other buildings of interest tucked away, and a 'town trail' is available either at the Museum or at the excellent Information Centre in Lower Monk Street, which is also the Brecon Beacons National Park Centre and well worth a visit.

Abergavenny is now a centre for many outdoor pursuits and there are many walks in the neighbourhood. The best guide to them is the National Park pamphlet *Thirty walks in the Abergavenny area*. The walk to the

---

PLACES OF INTEREST IN AND AROUND CRICKHOWELL

Grahame Amey Ltd, The Granary, Standard Street
Hand-made furniture workshop in historic building. Visitors welcome. Items for sale.

Curt-y-Gollen Barracks, 2½m south-east of Crickhowell on A40
Regimental museum of South Wales Borderers and other Welsh units.

Tretower Court and Castle, 3m north-west of Crickhowell on A479
Early fortified manor house and castle keep.

2
*

summit of the Sugar Loaf has long been a favourite excursion, and the easiest way is to leave the town on the A40 and after about a mile turn right into a road signposted 'Sugar Loaf'. You eventually reach a car park from which the final ascent of nearly two miles can be made.

4½
**

A less-frequented alternative is the track that is clearly marked on the OS map beginning at GR 291155. It passes round the eastern side of Rholben hill, but there is also a path over the top.

2½
*

The village of Fforest, four miles to the north of Abergavenny at GR 287206, is a good base for several walks to the north of the Sugar Loaf. One that should not be missed takes in the almost inaccessible church of Partrishow (pronounced 'Patricia'), possibly the best of many fascinating churches in the area. You cross the river Grwyne Fawr at GR 284211, branch right and take the track leading north from Pen-y-bair. The church is about a mile beyond.

Partrishow church is most famous for its superb rood loft and screen, but there are several other features of interest, including a 'memento mori' (a representation of Death as a skeleton) and three altar tables dating from before the Reformation. One of them is in a small cell at the west end. The inscription on the large font refers to Cynhillin, Prince of Powys just before the Norman Conquest, and seems to date it as eleventh century. Stone benches along the outside of the church facing the churchyard cross are a reminder that local affairs were once formally discussed at the cross. Close by is a stone hut with a fireplace where the priest could thaw out before taking the service.

The route out of Abergavenny is the A40 along the Usk valley, passing after four miles the former depot of the South Wales Borderers. It is now the headquarters of the Prince of Wales' Division, and its interesting museum can be visited. Crickhowell, two miles further on, lies under the distinctive flat-

Crickhowell Bridge, with 'Table Mountain' beyond

topped hill known as 'Table Mountain'. The slight remains of its castle are incorporated into a park on the left as you enter from this direction. The tiny square has the decorative Bear Hotel on one side; on the other, the High Street leads away towards the river and continues as Bridge Street, a most attractive hill with some well-maintained small houses.

The 13-arch stone bridge with pedestrian alcoves is the pride of Crickhowell, and the river can be an exciting sight here when it is in full spate. You get a good view of the town from the bridge, and the church is particularly prominent. If you walk back up by the main road instead of Bridge Street, you can see at the top an impressive old wall with a gatehouse. This is Porth Mawr, and used to be the entrance to an important Tudor house belonging to the Herbert family. Unfortunately the house has been long since demolished.

The Crickhowell Community Council have produced a 'trail' for the town which can be obtained locally. If you want to climb Table Mountain the best way is probably via the lane at Glannant (GR 214191). You turn on to a lane to the right very shortly after, and then take the track to the left after a quarter of a mile. The large white house to the

north-west is Gwernvale, the birthplace of Sir George Everest. He was the first to map accurately the position of the mountain to which he gave his name.

Two miles beyond Crickhowell the road forks and you take the A479, which quickly brings you to Tretower. From the main road you can see at once the castle and manor house down on the left. The castle was once of great importance, lying as it did at the junction of routes west to Brecon and north to Hay. Originally made of wood, it was surrounded by a stone curtain wall in the twelfth century, and, not long after, the old buildings were replaced by the present circular tower. A little later still, the adjoining Tretower Court was built, presumably to provide more comfortable accommodation.

The buildings are open to the public and worth a visit. Before going in, notice the fine restored stone barn opposite the gateway; inside, the castle has become inextricably mixed up with a farm, which somehow seems preferable to the neat municipalisation at Abergavenny.

Soon after Tretower the hills begin to close in on each side of the road. Pen Tir and the Mynydd Troed range on the left are very prominent, while high up on the right is the craggy escarpment of Mynydd Llysiau at over two thousand

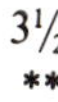

3½
**

feet. Then the countryside suddenly opens up at Pengenffordd and there is a gentle descent into Talgarth.

The car park here is in what was once the station yard, and traces of the old Brecon, Hay and Hereford railway, mentioned often in the Kilvert Diaries, can still be seen. Three miles north, near Three Cocks, was a junction with a line that ran up the Wye valley and on past Rhayader. Talgarth is rather austere, although picturesque enough with its steep and narrow streets. One interesting feature in the square is a medieval tower and guardhouse by the bridge, with a shop and bank neatly fitted into it. The church is at the north-east edge of the town and is dedicated, unusually, to St Gwendoline. Here there is a very significant memorial to Howell Harris, born nearby at Trefecca in 1713.

The story of Howell Harris and the 'Family' is a fascinating one, too long to be told in full here. He was the founder of the Calvinistic Methodist Church of Wales and led a tough life of preaching, often at odds with the Church of England and rival Nonconformist sects. Later in life he decided to establish a community, or Family, for his followers, who would give up their possessions and become self-supporting.

He set it up at Trefecca, and, surprisingly, it was a success, spreading to nearly eight hundred acres and proving to be well in the forefront of agricultural development at that time. Among other things Harris introduced into Wales the use of root crops as fodder and helped to found the Brecknockshire Agricultural Society, the first of its kind in Britain. Shortly before his death in 1773, a training college for ministers was added to the community. The buildings are still there, just over a mile to the south along the B4560, and the chapel block now houses an

PLACES OF INTEREST IN AND AROUND TALGARTH

George Dear Pottery, Upper Lion, Talgarth
Colourful stoneware. Visitors welcome.

Black Mountain Pottery, Llanelieu Court, 2½m east of Talgarth
Domestic stoneware, also drawings and paintings. Interesting church nearby.

Bronllys Malthouse, 1½m north-west of Talgarth
Built in 1885, open to public but not working. Full range of equipment, machinery and tools. Cafe.

Trefecca College, 1½m south of Talgarth on B4560
Home of former community set up by Howell Harris, Nonconformist preacher and agricultural pioneer. Museum relating to Harris's life and work.

interesting Harris museum.

If you visit Trefecca it is worth continuing south to Llangorse lake. Not so long ago, it was a lonely, romantic stretch of water supposedly concealing a submerged town, but in recent years it has attracted camping and caravan sites, a holiday adventure centre and various water sports facilities. Visited out of season it provides much of interest in the way of wildlife. A waymarked path round the western side links Llangorse in the north with Llangasty in the south.

Across the river from Talgarth is Bronllys, noted for a church with a very odd detached tower and also for its big hospital, built with funds raised as a memorial to Edward VII. The castle here consists of little more than a high circular tower dating from the mid-thirteenth century. Access to the main chamber is possible by way of a wooden staircase, and the basement and dungeon can be inspected from above, but there is no way to the top.

The A4078 out of Talgarth leads on to Three Cocks and Glasbury, and you begin to enter the Kilvert country. When the diaries of Francis Kilvert were published just before the Second World War, they were recognised at once not only as a literary classic but as a valuable source of social history. This young, susceptible clergyman, who was curate of Clyro in the 1870s brought a fresh and observant eye to the comings and goings in his part of the countryside. Each year people come to Clyro to retrace Kilvert's walks and visits, and a Society exists to encourage this interest.

The bridge at Glasbury marks the reunion with the river Wye, and this village has suffered more than most during its history from severe flooding. This explains the fact that the church is a long way from the village; it was built out of harm's way in 1664, after the original building had been washed away. The present church is a new version, built on the same site in 1836.

There is an interesting walk in the hills to the east here. The starting point is the path from the main road at GR 168372. It goes east to join a minor road close to 'Old Gwernyfed', a Tudor house with a fascinating history told in detail in a pamphlet published by Powys County Council and available from most information centres in Powys. It is not open to the public but can be viewed from the road. From nearby Felindre take the track that runs south over Bychan Common; when you reach another minor road turn right and then left to visit Llanelieu church. It is a simple building in a fine setting. Its most interesting feature is the roughly-carved rood screen, rather less sophisticated than others in this area but adding much to the austere and remote atmosphere of the church. If it is locked, the key can normally be obtained from the farm close by. The return route is to Ffostill and then the track beginning at GR 183347.

After crossing the river at Glasbury and continuing on the A438 you see after a mile a left turn signposted 'Maesyronnen Chapel'. It is one of the very earliest places of Nonconformist worship in Wales — a low, single-storey building with a tiny cottage at one end. It is usually locked, but by peering through the windows you can see that much of the original furnishing remains, including the extremely uncomfortable wooden benches.

Nearby Llowes has a church notable for its Celtic Cross and a common that was one of Kilvert's favourite walks. From here it is three miles to Clyro, which seems to have changed remarkably little since Kilvert's time, apart from the by-pass, which has taken the traffic out of the village but is definitely a visual intrusion. As you turn off into the village, you see on the other side of the by-pass the old school where Kilvert taught. To find his lodgings you turn right at the church gate. The house, once known as Ty Dulas and now called Ashbrook, is solid but unremarkable apart from its plaque. The Baskerville Arms, frequently mentioned by Kilvert who used its old name, the Swan, still stands opposite, and the noise is no doubt just as irritating to the present occupiers of Ashbrook as it was to Kilvert.

A good guide to the village can be bought in the church, and anyone wishing to find out more should read

After Kilvert by A L Le Quesne. Mr Le Quesne, a devotee of the Diaries, decided to move to the Clyro area, discovered that Kilvert's house happened to be on the market and moved in. His book has a lot to tell about Clyro in Kilvert's day and his own a hundred years later.

He makes the point that to the motorist Hay-on-Wye is a few minutes' drive across the bridge; in the 1870s a shopping trip to the town was a major expedition for the inhabitants of Clyro. Opinions differ on the subject of Hay. For some people it is an undistinguished jumble of nondescript architecture and claustrophobic streets; for others it is the perfect small town with an intimate and convivial atmosphere. It does give the impression of being built on a miniature scale, and there is a strong sense of a medieval town huddling at the foot of its castle.

Not so long ago Hay was like most other small border towns — a rural shopping centre and market. Now it has achieved wider fame as 'the world's biggest bookshop'. Richard Booth first set up shop in the Castle, and since then he has extended his empire to many other buildings in the town, including the former cinema and fire station. 'The Castle' is something of a misnomer — very few traces remain of the Norman structure. The building that occupies the site is a seventeenth-century mansion, occupied in Kilvert's time by the Bevan family with whom he spent a good deal of time. The motte of a smaller and earlier castle can be seen between the town centre and the rather distant church of St Mary, which was almost entirely rebuilt in 1834. You can buy a detailed 'town trail' in the church.

The modern bridge is the latest of a series since 1763 which have been destroyed by flooding, ice or other disasters. The Wye has proved a mixed blessing, although it was once a source of commercial prosperity for the town. There is now an attractive walk along its bank, reached by a path near the church.

Hay is undoubtedly one of the best touring centres in the border region, lying as it does at the meeting-place of three characteristic border landscapes — the mountains to the south, the Radnor moorlands to the north, and the rich Herefordshire countryside to the west.

8 The Lower Wye Valley and The Forest of Dean

A good starting point for a tour of these two very different areas is Ross-on-Wye. The town sits at the end of the M50, but a by-pass has relieved it of much of the traffic that used to plague it. The Wye loops sharply here, and the best view of Ross is from the bank below, from which pleasant buildings rise in terraces towards St Mary's church with its elegant spire.

The dominant figure in the history of Ross was John Kyrle, celebrated as the 'Man of Ross' in some of Alexander Pope's less inspired verse. He was obviously a remarkable man. Much of the town's present layout is his work, and in the course of his 87 years from 1637 to 1724 he was responsible for countless charitable acts that endeared him to the local population.

The seventeenth-century Market Hall, an unassuming sandstone building, stands at the head of the bustling Broad Street. On its north wall is a carving of a heart and the letters FC, signifying 'faithful to Charles in heart' — a device expressing Kyrle's intense monarchism and placed there so that he could see it from his house opposite. The house itself is now divided into a shop and offices, and in the garden behind is Kyrle's summerhouse.

Oddly enough, no memorial was erected to Kyrle until fifty years after his death, when the large monument was placed in the sanctuary of the church. St Mary's is a light and spacious building, dating basically from the thirteenth century, and a good deal of the glass in the east window is original. There are some notable memorials here apart from

Kyrle's, including the one to the Rudhall family, who were also benefactors of the town.

The churchyard contains an interesting cross commemorating over 300 victims of an epidemic of the plague in 1637 — the plague pit was close by. The Prospect, a public garden, lies west of the churchyard and is the starting point of Kyrle's Walk, a path which he supplied with trees and seats. These seem to have been the victims of early vandalism, or simply the desire of successive parish priests for firewood.

The centre of Ross is harmonious, with few outstanding individual buildings, although the sixteenth-century Rudhall Almshouses in Church Street are worth seeing, as are the Webbe's Almshouses of a century later in Copse Cross Street.

To start the journey down the Wye Valley you make for the A40 to Monmouth, crossing Wilton Bridge just outside the town. This riverside area has been pleasantly landscaped, and Wilton Castle (not open) stands nearby. The busy main road follows the Wye for about four miles, when the river swings away towards Goodrich. A minor road branches off to follow it, and this brings you into the village past 'Ye Olde Hostelrie' — a pub that is in fact a turreted folly.

Since there is no parking space in Goodrich you will need to pay to get into the picnic site next to the castle. This is a most impressive ruin in sandstone, rising from solid rock. The twelfth-century keep is the oldest portion — the remainder is at least a

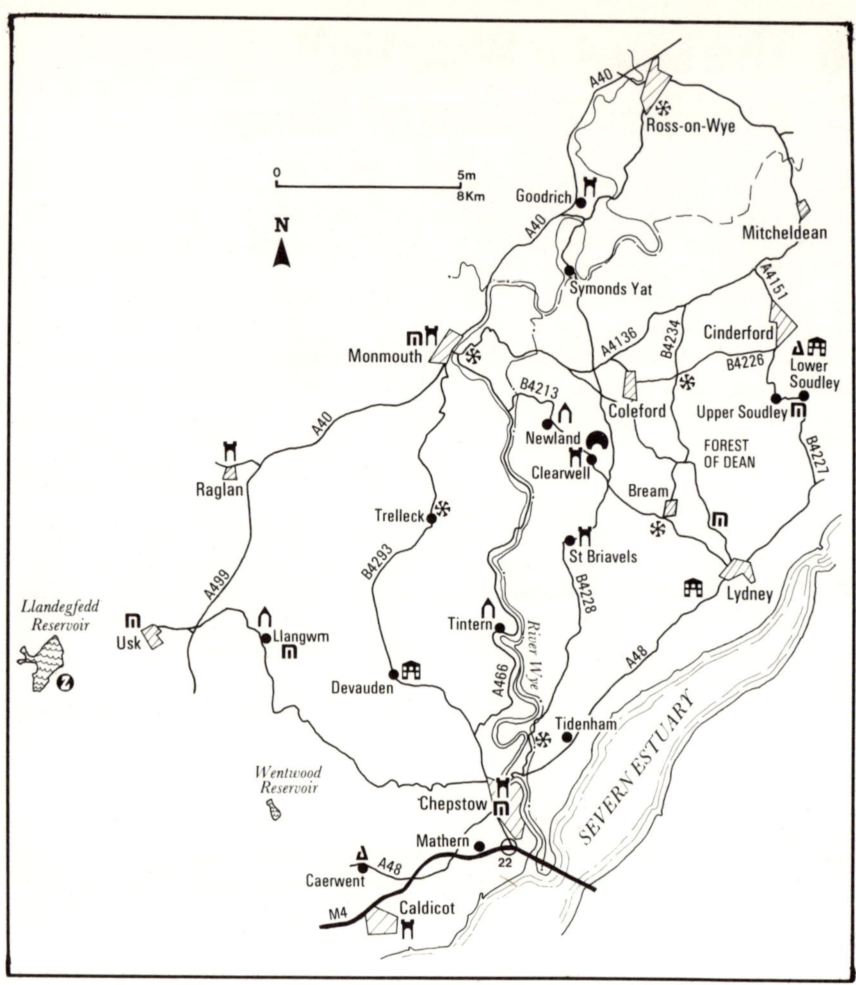

century newer. One of the more interesting features inside is the small chapel that once had a rood-loft. The castle remained virtually intact until the Civil War, when it was ruined by Parliamentary siege forces.

If you leave Goodrich by the B4229 you will arrive after half a mile at a narrow road signposted Symonds Yat East. It is one way up to the famous viewpoint, crossing the river and passing over a flat expanse with Coppet Hill to the left, Huntsham Hill in front, and over to the right the scattered hillside dwellings of Great Doward. Continue uphill when the road forks until you reach the Forestry Commission car park. The Yat Rock is a few hundred yards away.

As a tourist attraction it may be hackneyed but the view from the rock is no less remarkable. Down below there appear to be two parallel rivers. They are, of course, both the Wye, and what you see are the beginning and end of a huge loop concealed from view by

Goodrich Castle

The Wye from Symonds Yat

Huntsham Hill.

After re-joining the A40 there is little to stop for before Monmouth, which deserves a long stay. It is worth noting that parking is not easy, and it is advisable to make for the first car park you see signposted.

Coming from Ross you enter the town from the 'wrong' end, and the thing to do is to walk immediately down Monnow Street to the one surviving thirteenth-century gatehouse incorporated into the Monnow Bridge — an almost unique defensive feature, last pressed into service during the Chartist unrest.

The small arches on each side were made to accommodate pavements when the road was widened in the nineteenth century. The suburb of Over Monnow has its own attractions, one of them being the church of St Thomas next to the bridge, originally Norman and heavily restored, but still boasting a superb original chancel arch.

A leisurely walk back along Monnow Street will reveal a pleasant mixture of unpretentious architecture with the best buildings on the right hand side, in particular the Robin Hood Inn, Chippenham House and Cornwall House. At the top of the street the buildings of the old town centre close tightly in, squashed as they are by the bottleneck formed by the Wye on one side and its tributary the Monnow on the other.

Agincourt Square is the heart of the town, dominated by the eighteenth-century Shire Hall, the site of the street market. The name of the square is a reminder that Henry V was born in the castle here in 1387, and a rather coy statue of him occupies a niche on the front of the Hall. Monmouth's other famous local boy, Charles Rolls, is remembered in more robust fashion by a statue at ground level, showing the motoring and aviation pioneer studying a model plane with some satisfaction. The Shire Hall is flanked by two fine old pubs, the King's Head and the Beaufort Arms.

Behind the square to the west are the ruins of the castle and also the magnificent Great Castle House. Only the remnants of the Great Tower and the Great Hall are visible on the castle site, and the seventeenth-century house is much more interesting. Unfortunately they can only be visited by special arrangement, being occupied by the Royal Monmouthshire Royal Engineers, a Territorial unit that has some claim to be the oldest in existence.

The curving Priory Street contains the Market Hall, a classical building dating from the 1830s but rebuilt in the 1960s after a fire. It now houses two very interesting museums. One is devoted to

Monnow Bridge gatehouse, Monmouth

local history and tradition while the other is a collection of Nelson relics donated to the town by the mother of Charles Rolls.

The church of St Mary is not particularly distinguished — it is a nineteenth-century reconstruction of an eighteenth-century reconstruction — and its most graceful feature is probably the slender spire. This part of the town repays a close inspection of its handsome, small-scale architecture.

The by-pass may have made the town more pleasant to walk in, but it has also ruined the frontage to the Wye, because the massive embankment of the A40 effectively seals Monmouth off from the river. However, the road does not succeed in dominating the Gothic architecture of Monmouth School opposite the bridge by which you leave to resume the drive down the Wye.

The road is the A466, which at this point runs along the fringe of the Forest of Dean, passing first through Redbrook. There is little to see here now, although it was once an important industrial settlement. After Redbrook you drive along a fine wooded valley before crossing the river at the elegant Bigsweir bridge, a convenient point of access to the path that runs along the left bank. On the Welsh side of the bridge a minor road turns off to Whitebrook, noted for its papermills, some of which can still be seen converted into houses. Opposite this turning is the site of a riverside railway station — a relic of the Wye Valley line that followed the river closely.

At Llandogo, a mile further on, you may well be put off by the commercialised road frontage, but it is in fact a village with a fascinating history as the upper limit of tidal navigation. It was here that the cargoes of boats that had sailed from Chepstow were transferred to shallow-draught barges hauled by large teams of men. Several of the gravestones in the churchyard are adorned with anchors and there is still a nautical air about the place. There is access from the village to various viewpoints and picnic sites in the woods above.

Two miles from Llandogo there is a lay-by on the right — your only chance to park in order to visit the riverside settlement of Brockweir on the other bank. It is a picturesque place now with its wharves, old houses and Moravian chapel, and it is hard to believe that it once ranked next to Chepstow as a Wye port and was noted for its shipbuilding. The river trade declined with the coming of the railway and Brockweir is now a quiet residential village.

A few hundred yards after Brockweir look out for a lane to the left leading to Tintern station. The station has been imaginatively restored, complete with station building, signal box, signals, length of track and a coach. The signal box houses a useful information centre and refreshments are available in a

Bigsweir Bridge, Wye Valley

---

waiting-room full of railway relics.

After this it is only a short distance to the valley's most famous attraction, though much of the magic of Tintern Abbey has been dissipated by the garishness of the adjacent village and the commercialism of the site itself. However, if you turn your back on the cafe and gift shop it is still possible to appreciate the splendid ruins, especially from inside the ruined nave. The first Abbey was built here in 1131, but the present building dates from the late thirteenth century and is still in a remarkable state of preservation. After the Dissolution a metal works was set up on the site, and a plaque on the wall records the fact that brass was first successfully made here.

The road now begins to climb steadily, and at the point where it emerges from the woodland at the top there is a minor road on the right leading to the Wynd Cliff, a celebrated viewpoint. The area is now managed by the Forestry Commission which has set up a picnic site and nature trail, but the most famous feature here is the steep path, created in 1829, known as the 365 steps.

The big racecourse on the left indicates that you are approaching Chepstow. It is a town with a long history as a port and ship-building centre, and although little evidence of it remains today the most interesting part of the town is still the area that lies within the loop of the Wye.

From the Town Gate the handsome and cheerful High Street slopes down to Beaufort Square, from which narrower thoroughfares lead down to the river. The Square is still the natural focal point of the town, and there is space to sit and decide which way to go next.

To the east Station Road leads to the former shipyard area and a fine converted flour mill. The cobbled Hocker Hill Street has some of the most picturesque buildings, including the eighteenth-century Powis Almshouses, while St Mary Street is a mellow blend of

Crickhowell bridge over the river Usk

The Wye from Symonds Yat

Llandegfedd Reservoir, near Usk

Goodrich Castle

old and new shop fronts with interesting upper storeys. The two latter roads both take you to Church Street, which has the very large parish church at its east end. It has to be said that the church, fairly ruthlessly altered in the nineteenth century, has little to distinguish it apart from a decorated Norman doorway left in the eighteenth-century tower.

By going down Lower Church Street you reach 'The Back' — the riverside area that was the centre of Chepstow's commercial life as a port. The steep limestone cliffs opposite catch the eye, as does the railway bridge. Brunel built the original in 1852 as a suspension bridge, and although a new central span was installed in the 1960s his bold iron columns remain. The superb iron road bridge has survived much longer, having been built in 1816.

The castle comes into view here, sprawling alongside the river on its long, narrow site. It is a huge structure, and the earliest section, the Great Tower, is unusual in having been constructed in stone in very early Norman times. The castle was progessively enlarged and strengthened, although the defences were not really tested until the Civil War, when the Parliamentarians besieged and eventually captured it. No extensive damage resulted and it was inhabited up to the present century.

You reach the entrance by walking up Bridge Street. The small Chepstow Museum is immediately opposite the castle gate, and Bridge Street itself boasts a fine terrace of early nineteenth-century houses.

It is not often that a town itinerary includes the main car park, but Chepstow's is rather different. Not only is it a good vantage point for a striking close-up view of the castle but it is bounded by a stretch of the thirteenth-century Portwall, which originally sealed off the town on the landward side. It connects with the Town Gate and continues even more impressively on the other side, running past the 'garden suburb' of Hardwick, an interesting early experiment in the use of concrete for housebuilding.

The area to the south-west, now effectively cut off by the M4, is low-lying and fairly nondescript in character, but there are three places of interest in the Newport direction that can be visited in the course of an afternoon.

By leaving Chepstow on the A48, crossing the motorway and turning left on to the B4245 you can get to Caldicot. It is a dull town in itself, but tucked away behind the housing estates is the castle, originally twelfth century and restored with some skill in the nineteenth. The buildings are extensive and the gatehouse is especially impressive — regular medieval banquets are held in the hall above it. The surrounding park is freely accessible.

Caerwent, to the north of Caldicot, was the Roman town of Venta Silurum, and its present buildings sit casually among some remarkable remains. The most obvious feature is the extensive wall, over 15ft high in places, but right next to the main street are the foundations of a temple, incongruously surrounded by caravans.

Continue west along the A48 and you arrive at Penhow, where the castle (inhabited and rather different from the others in the neighbourhood) is now a major tourist attraction, with elaborate visual and auditory aids for the visitor.

To the north-west of Chepstow the country is high, clear and invigorating, and although the Usk lacks the drama of the Wye it has been far less commercialised.

The way out is the B4235 to Usk, which after five miles passes the

Chepstow Castle

PLACES OF INTEREST IN AND AROUND CHEPSTOW

Castle, Entrance in Bridge Street
Very large site, earliest section dating from twelfth century.

Museum, Bridge Street
Local history collection.

Brockweir, Wyeside settlement 6m north of Chepstow
Former port and shipbuilding centre.

Tintern Station, off A466 5½m north of Chepstow
Restored station of former Wye Valley Railway. Museum, picnic site, information centre.

Tintern Abbey, beside A466 5½m north of Chepstow
Splendid remains of extensive Cistercian abbey.

Wynd Cliff, off A466 2½m north of Chepstow
Fine viewpoint, picnic site, walks (including '365 steps').

Caldicot Castle, 5m south-west of Chepstow
Castle remains, country park, frequent medieval banquets.

Caerwent, 6m west of Chepstow on A48
Roman town, extensive walls and foundations of temple.

Penhow Castle, 9m west of Chepstow on A48
Inhabited castle. Guided tours with video information etc.

Beaufort Aviaries, at Devauden, 5m north-west of Chepstow on B4293
Pheasants, tropical birds, rabbits etc.

130

Wentwood Forest to the left. There are the usual picnic sites and forest trails here, with the additional attraction of the Wentwood Reservoir where fishing is possible.

At Llangwm a right turn leads to Wolvesnewton, where the model farm and folk collection are likely to be of special interest to children. There is a craft centre and a programme of temporary exhibitions during the summer. If you take the left turn in Llangwm you will reach the Gwent Ski Centre, which sounds unlikely until you realise that the skiing is on grass. All the necessary equipment can be hired.

A few hundred yards beyond this crossroads is an inconspicuous right turn at the top of the hill. It leads to Llangwm's two churches. The first, St John's, is small, simple and unremarkable, but St Jerome's, a short distance further along the lane, is surprisingly large, with a magnificent tower and the finest rood screen in the area. Equally attractive is the little church at Gwernesney, situated just before the point where the B4235 crosses the A449.

Usk is smaller than you might expect. Best known for its fishing and its agricultural college, it does not go out of its way to attract tourists, although the Rural Life Museum in Newmarket Street makes an interesting stop. The church, too, should be visited — it has a famous and splendid organ, bought from Llandaff Cathedral in 1899. The castle is privately owned, but the ruins of the Priory are freely accessible next to the church. On the far side of the bridge carrying the Pontypool road is the picnic site known as 'The Island', and a locally-produced pamphlet details several walks from it.

The left turn on the other side of this bridge (signposted Llanbadoc) leads to

the Llandegfedd Reservoir, where boats can be hired and where there is a farm park with rare breeds, vintage machinery and an adventure playground.

There is a direct road from Usk to Raglan and its famous castle (it is best to avoid the A449). Having been built in the fifteenth century — unusually late — Raglan Castle is a sophisticated structure, designed to resist cannon balls rather than arrows. The Great Tower is a castle within a castle, having its own moat and planned as a final place of refuge. In fact the castle developed into a comfortable residence, and the most serious action there was in 1646 when it was captured by Parliamentary forces and systematically ruined. There is still a great deal to see and a visit is highly recommended.

The scenic route back to Chepstow is the B4293, a turning off the A40 just before Monmouth. Five miles along it is Trellech, once a very important town and therefore possessing an unusually large church. A very old preaching cross is prominent in the churchyard, and inside there is a curious seventeenth-century sundial showing Trellech's three tourist attractions — the Harold Stones (origin unknown) that stand in a field on the left of the B4293 to the south of the village, a Norman motte called The Tump in a farmyard to the south-west of the church, and the Virtuous Well (probably an early spa) just outside the village on the left of the minor road to Tintern.

There is now an enjoyable drive back to Chepstow, although anyone interested in birds will want to stop at Devauden to visit the Beaufort Aviaries, where, in addition to a collection of pheasants and exotic birds, there is a large rabbit colony guaranteed to round off the day for most children.

The Forest of Dean
The Forest of Dean is an intricate area with tremendous scope for the walker. As a Forest Park it has been sympathetically developed for recreation, and its well-charted paths provide a whole range of expeditions, from short family rambles to more serious long-distance walks.

It would be superfluous to detail the walks in this chapter. The Ramblers' Association provide leaflets for the longer ones, while the Forestry Commission publishes guides to forest trails and accessible beauty spots. In addition there is an invaluable pamphlet issued by Gwent County Council showing parking places and other facilities for holidaymakers. Also recommended is H.W. Paar's pamphlet *An industrial tour of the Wye Valley and the Forest of Dean*, which provides a clear guide to the wealth of old industrial sites and relics in the Forest.

Since the long-stay visitor is so well provided with literature, the rest of this chapter is designed for those with limited time who want to sample the Forest's unique atmosphere.

Monmouth is a suitable starting point, and the way out is the A4136. Very soon after crossing the river and branching left you need to look out for a concealed right turn that will take you up to the Kymin. This is yet another famous viewpoint, but it has an odd additional feature — the 'Naval Temple', bearing the names of sixteen British admirals. If you miss the turn to the Kymin you can stop at a parking place on the right $1\frac{1}{2}$m further on and walk up to the Buckstone, which commands an equally fine view.

Staunton is the first village along this road, and its wind-swept church is well worth a visit. Among other features is a pulpit with a staircase leading from it up to a former rood loft, and its sanctuary is detached from the rest of the church by the central tower and the bell-ringing area beneath.

Shortly after the village take the B4431 to the right. This leads to Coleford, one of the small, functional towns characteristic of the Forest. There is nothing obviously picturesque here, unless it is the sight of an isolated church tower dividing the traffic in the town centre. The Angel Hotel is a striking coaching inn, and also one of the few places around here where you can get a cup of coffee.

Coleford is a convenient centre for one or two short expeditions. About four miles due east on the B4226 is the famous Speech House, built in 1676 as a

courthouse for the Foresters of Dean. It
was known as the Court of Verderers,
and it still meets theoretically every forty
days, although in practice the four
Verderers hold business meetings
quarterly to carry out their duties, less
concerned now with justice than with the
safeguarding of the environment.

A short distance back along the
Coleford road is the car park for the
Speech House forest trail, and by
turning down the minor road beside the
House you quickly reach the New Fancy
trail, which takes in railway as well as
natural history. The return to Coleford
can be made by the B4431.

North of the town the B4432 is an
alternative route to Symonds Yat and
also to the various forest trails and
picnic sites in Highmeadow Woods. To
the south there are two notable
attractions that can be reached by taking
the St Briavels road and branching left
after less than two miles at the
Lambsquay Hotel.

The Clearwell Caves, a short way
along this road, are in fact a group of
eight caverns, part of a network of
former iron mines. It is possible to go
underground to see the workings, and
there are also displays of machinery and
equipment. By continuing along the
same road to Clearwell village and
turning left at the church you arrive at
Clearwell castle. It is something of an
oddity, dating from the early 1700s and
claiming to be the first example of the
craze for mock-Gothic architecture. It is
now being restored for the second time
and its attractions (designed mainly for
family outings) include a restaurant.

The visit to Clearwell can be rounded
off by travelling the 2m north-west to
Newland. Newland church is known as
'The Cathedral of the Forest', a title
earned not so much by its size as by its
open interior, which gives the effect of

great spaciousness. The resemblance to a
cathedral is reinforced by the number of
memorials and small chapels. A useful
guidebook, available in the church,
details the many unusual features, the
most famous of which is the 'Miner's
Brass' in the Greyndour Chapel. It is
believed to be the family crest and shows
in remarkable detail the figure of a
medieval forest miner with a hod and
pick and holding a candle in his mouth.
The attractive William Jones
almshouses by the side of the church
have superb stone tile roofs and date
from 1615.

The route now continues south to St
Briavels, a quiet village in an impressive
position high above the Wye. The
church is interesting, but more
unexpected is the thirteenth-century
castle, part of which now serves as a
youth hostel. The two round gatehouse
towers catch the eye, but there are
residential buildings behind and the
remains of a large moat. In its time it has
been a courthouse and prison, but there
is no record of any military action here.

An unusual church is the main
attraction at Hewelsfield, 2m to the
south. The nave dates from Saxon times
and the Normans added a squat tower.
The chancel was added still later, and
the result, as at Staunton, was to
distance the sanctuary from the
congregation. The exterior is dominated
by the sweep of the nave roof, which
extends almost to the ground.

So far the B4228 has not been of great
interest, but it now starts to pass
through high woodland with occasional
glimpses of the Severn estuary. In fact
there is a picnic site and viewpoint $2\frac{1}{2}$m
from Hewelsfield, and 3m further on is
the famous Wintour's Leap. There is no
official parking place here and you can
easily miss it, so it is worth stopping
where you can and walking to see this

200ft precipice, supposedly jumped on horseback by Sir John Wintour in 1642 when escaping from the Parliamentarians.

To avoid arriving back in Chepstow you need to take either the lane just before the Leap or the one after down towards the estuary to Tidenham. The church here has a Norman lead font and is also of interest because its tower once served as a navigation beacon for shipping. The lane through Tidenham meets the A48, and you turn left and start to travel parallel to the estuary shore towards Lydney.

This is a dull road, and there are few good reasons for leaving it, unless it is to visit the intersting churches at Woolaston and Alvington, both very close to the road. The last village before Lydney is Aylburton, which is dominated by Lydney Park. The Park is occasionally open in the summer months, and it is worth a phone call to find out, because in addition to the splendid gardens and deer there is a Roman site with a museum of excavated objects.

Lydney is a busy modern town, and its main attraction for the visitor lies a mile to the north on the B4234. It is the Norchard Steam Centre, run by the Dean Forest Railway members, who generously open their yard and allow

enthusiasts to roam freely round their
remarkable collection of locomotives
and rolling stock in various stages of
restoration. From June to September
short steam trips are possible on
Sundays.

Bream, 3m north-west of Lydney, is
famous for its Roman iron workings
known as The Scowles. They are buried
in the middle of thick woodland on the
left just before you enter the village, but
the public path starts in the village itself
(OS599053).

The A48 now runs direct to Blakeney,
but a more attractive route is the B4234
past the Steam Centre, branching on to
the B4431 at Parkend, a community rich
in industrial history. (H.W. Paar covers
this in detail, together with a wealth of
other information about this south-east
corner of the Forest that was once so
heavily industrialised). Three miles after
Parkend a section of Roman road has
been uncovered at Blackpool Bridge
(OS653087).

On reaching Blakeney you turn north
again almost at once on the B4227 to
pass through the spectacular Soudley
Valley, which can be appreciated even
by those not interested in industrial
history. The Dean Heritage Museum by
the road on the northern outskirts of
Lower Soudley is dedicated to the
history and traditions of the forest, and
its central feature is an old watermill.

The long sprawl of Ruspidge merges
imperceptibly into Cinderford, now a
country town but once a centre of the
mining industry. It has the utilitarian
look of most Forest towns and there is
little to catch the eye, but the
surrounding countryside is not without
interest.

At Littledean, on the A4151 to the
east, is Dean Hall, a building that is
claimed to span over 800 years of
architectural history. Roman and Saxon
traces have been found, and excavation
is still going on. Quite apart from the
interest of the building the grounds are
extremely attractive. From here it is only
a short distance to Newnham, a pleasant
place right on the edge of the Servern
and with a church commanding a fine
view across the river. One of the best
buildings here is the seventeenth-century
inn opposite the church.

Moving north from Cinderford on the
A4151 you reach the crossroads at
Nailbridge and make for Mitcheldean.
The old spoilheaps in the field below
Harrow Hill Church are very noticeable
from the crossroads and typical of the
area.

In spite of the usual spread of modern
housing Mitcheldean retains a good deal
of character, with some half-timbered
houses and a huge church with
exceptionally fine roofs. A wooden
screen between nave and chancel
contains Tudor paintings of the Last
Judgement, while the immense reredos
has life-size marble figures.

While in Mitcheldean do not overlook
the church at Abenhall (or Abinghall).
This is a very old coalmining centre
reached by way of a minor road south
from the centre of Mitcheldean. The
main treasure of the isolated church is a
fifteenth-century octagonal font,
presented by the Free Smiths and Guild
of Miners and bearing their arms.

As a final memory of the Forest you
might like to climb the 1000ft May Hill
to the north-west of Mitcheldean. The
simplest way to reach it is to follow the
A4136, turn left at the junction with the
A40 and into the village of Dursley
Cross. A minor road from here brings
you to the public footpath to the
summit, which has extensive views to the
south.

After this there is little to stop for on
the short journey back to Ross-on-Wye.

Long Distance Footpaths

When using long distance paths, always carry a map — the waymarking is seldom as clear as it might be, and if the path has not been heavily used it may at times disappear.

The *Glyndwr Way* is a 120m walk which begins and ends in the border area. The starting point is Knighton, and from there the path winds its way across to Machynlleth before returning via Lake Vyrnwy to Welshpool. It passes through some of the best parts of north and mid-Powys, and is easy to use in short stretches because the Powys County Council have issued sixteen leaflets, each covering a length of 7-10m. They are excellent value for money, each one forming the basis for a rewarding day out.

Lower Wye Valley Walk. This walk follows the river closely, running from Hereford to Chepstow and covering about fifty miles. It runs through, or near, many of the most famous attractions of the lower Wye Valley. There is a warden service. A leaflet and set of strip maps are available from Information Centres or from Mr M.J. Perry, County Hall, Cwmbran, Gwent NP44 2XH.

The *Offa's Dyke Path* runs from Prestatyn to Chepstow, a distance of about 140m. It provides the most varied walking of any of the long-distance paths of Britain, taking in mountains, moorland, river valleys and towns. Some stretches are undoubtedly dull, and the average walker will probably want to sample it at intervals rather than attempt the whole walk. Particularly recommended are the lengths over the Black Mountains, across the Radnor and Clun Forests and through the interesting countryside between Llanymynech and the Clwydian range. A set of large-scale strip maps, route notes and much other useful information can be obtained from the Offa's Dyke Association, West Street, Knighton, where there is also an information centre for visitors.

The *Wye Valley Walk* is less ambitious — 36m from Rhayader to Hay-on-Wye, following the course of the border's most beautiful river. Powys County Council have produced a set of four pamphlets as a guide to features of interest on the walk, and they can be obtained from the Planning Department at Llandrindod Wells or from local information centres.

Further Information

There are literally hundreds of castle sites in the Welsh border area, the majority of them consisting of little more than an earth mound. The following list includes only those castles where there are substantial ruins to be seen.

Caldicot
Tel: 0291 420241
Open: daily, March-October.

Chepstow (DOE)
Open: mid-March - mid-October, weekdays 9.30am-6.30pm, Sunday 2-4pm, April-September 9-30am-6.30pm; rest of year, weekdays 9.30am-4pm, Sunday 2-4pm.

Chirk (National Trust)
Tel: 0691 77791
Open: Easter-end May and October, Tuesday, Wednesday, Thursday and Sunday 2-5pm; June-September, Tuesday, Wednesday and Thursday 12 noon-5.30pm and Sunday 2-5.30pm; Bank Holiday Mondays 12 noon-5.30pm.

Cholmondeley
Near Whitchurch
Open: Easter-end September, Sunday and Bank Holidays 12 noon-6pm.

Clearwell
Tel: 0594 (Coleford) 32320
Open: Good Friday-October, daily except Sunday and Monday, 11am-5.30pm.

Croft (National Trust)
Near Leominster
Open: May-end September, Wednesday-Sunday and Bank Holiday Mondays 2-6pm; April and October, weekends and Easter Monday 2-6pm.

Goodrich (DOE) as for Chepstow

Ludlow
Open: May-end September, daily 10.30am-6pm; October-April, Monday-Saturday 10.30am-4.30pm.

Monmouth (DOE)
Open: visits by arrangement with the Adjutant, Royal Monmouthshire RE, Castle House.

Penhow
Tel: 0633 400800
Open: Easter-end September, Wednesday-Sunday and Bank Holidays, 10am-6pm.

Raglan (DOE)
As for Chepstow

St Briavels
Open: by arrangement with Youth Hostel Warden.

Shrewsbury
Tel: 0743 52019
Open: Easter-end September, daily 10am-5pm; October-Easter, Monday-Saturday 10am-4pm.

Stokesay
Open: April-end September, daily
except Monday (open Bank Holiday
Mondays) 10am-6pm; March and
October, daily except Monday 10am-
5pm; closed Tuesday in July and
August.

Tretower (DOE)
Open: May-end September, weekdays
9.30am-7pm, Sunday 2-7pm; March,
April and October, weekdays 9.30am-
5.30pm, Sunday 2-5.30pm; November-
February, weekdays 9.30am-4pm,
Sunday 2-4pm.

Usk
Open: by appointment only with owner,
Mr R.J. Humphreys, Castle House.

Welshpool (National Trust)
Tel: 0938 4336
Open: May-end September, daily except
Monday and Tuesday (open Bank
Holiday Mondays), castle 2-6pm,
gardens 1-6pm; gardens open every day
in July and August.

The following castles are freely
accessible at all reasonable times
without charge:
Abergavenny, Acton Burnell, Bronllys
(DOE), Clun, Grosmont (DOE),
Llangollen, Montgomery (DOE),
Moreton Corbet, Skenfrith (DOE),
White Castle (DOE), Whittington.

Adcote School
Little Ness, off A5 north-west of
Shrewsbury
Tel: 0939 (Baschurch) 260202
Mid-Victorian mansion by Norman
Shaw, built in sixteenth-century style.
The Great Hall is particularly
impressive.
Open: mid-April-mid-July and most of
September. It is advisable to telephone
the school secretary beforehand.

Attingham Park (National Trust)
Atcham, 4m south-east of Shrewsbury
Tel: 074 377 (Upton Magna) 343
Imposing mansion of late eighteenth
century. Very fine farmhouse and
decoration, landscaped park.
Open: Easter Sunday-end September,
Tuesday, Wednesday, Thursday,
Saturday, Sunday and Bank Holiday
Mondays 2-5.30pm.

Beaufort Aviaries
Devauden Green, 5m north-west of
Chepstow on B4293
Tel: 02915 (Wolves-Newton) 346
Rare pheasants, tropical birds, rabbits
and peacocks.
Refreshments, souvenirs, free car park.
Open: All year except Christmas day
11am-6pm.

Berrington Hall (National Trust)
Off A49 3m north of Leominster
Eighteenth-century mansion with much
original decoration and fine furniture.
Dairy and Victorian laundry.
Open: May-end September,
Wednesday-Saturday and Bank Holiday
Mondays 2-6pm; April and October,
weekends and Easter Monday 2.30-6pm.

Burford House Gardens
1m west of Tenbury Wells (north-east of
Leominster)
Tel: 0584 (Tenbury Wells) 810777
Famous gardens and nurseries
propagating rare plants.
Open: Monday-Friday 9am-5pm;
Saturday, March-November, 9am-5pm,
other months 9am-1pm; Sunday,
March-November 2-5pm.

Croft Castle (National Trust)
On B4362 4m north-west of Leominster
Tel: 056 885 (Yarpole) 246
Sixteenth century with gothic additions.
Good furniture and pictures, fine
grounds.
(See castle section for opening times.)

Burton Court
Eardisland, off A44 6m west of
Leominster
Tel: 054 47 (Pembridge) 231
Basically eighteenth century with
nineteenth-century additions, but a
fourteenth-century Great Hall.
Costumes, fairground models etc. Soft
fruit for sale.
Open: mid-May-mid-September,
Wednesday, Thursday, Saturday,
Sunday and Bank Holiday Mondays
2.30-6pm.

Dinmore Manor
Near Westhope, south of Leominster on
A49
Tel: 043 271 (Canon Pyon) 322
Sixteenth-century building with modern
additions. Chapel of Knights of St John
of Jerusalem.
Open: daily except Christmas day.

Heath House
Leintwardine
Tel: Mr S. Dale, 054 74364
Early seventeenth century, noted
staircase of c1700.
Open: by appointment only.

Hodnet Hall Gardens
Hodnet, 7m east of Wem
Tel: 063 084 202
Sixty acres of gardens, including
ornamental water gardens. Plants for
sale.
Open: Easter-end September, weekdays
2-5pm, Sunday and Bank Holiday
Mondays 12 noon-6pm.

Jubilee Maze
Symonds Yat
Tel: 0600 890655
Open: Good Friday-end October, daily
except Friday, 11am-5.30pm.

Littledean Hall
Cinderford, Forest of Dean
Tel: 0594 24213
Historic house and grounds.
Open: daily 2-6pm.

Lydney Park
Tel: 0594 42844
Gardens and deer park.
Open: Easter Sunday and Monday,
every Sunday and Bank Holiday in May
and late Spring Bank Holiday week.

Moccas Court
13m west of Hereford off A438
Classic eighteenth-century house. Fine
decoration and furniture.
Open: April-end September, Thursday
2-6pm.

Newent Falconry Centre
Boulsdon, 7m east of Ross
Tel: 0531 (Newent) 820286
Open: February-end November, daily
except Tuesday, 10.30am-5.30pm.

Plas Newydd
Llangollen
Tel: 0978 860234
Home of the 'Ladies of Llangollen'.
Open: daily from May-end September.

Puzzle Wood
1m from Coleford on Chepstow road
Tel: 0594 33187
Woodland walks, ancient iron workings.
Open: daily except Monday, 11am-7pm.

Shipton Hall
On B4368 8m east of Church Stretton
Sixteenth-century house, partly
modernised in 1769. Good staircase and
library, some Elizabethan panelling.
Collection of china.
Open: May-end September, Thursday
2.30-5.30pm; also Sunday in July and
August.

Stanwardine Hall
Ellesmere, on minor road off A528, just
south of Cockshutt
Tel: Mr D. Bridge 093 922 (Cockshutt)
212
3-storey Elizabethan mansion, now a
farmhouse.
Open: by appointment only.

Trelydan Hall 3m north of Welshpool
Tel: 0938 2773
Restored Tudor house. Costume
display, courses in floral arts and crafts
etc.
Open: for booked parties only.

Tyn-y-Rhos Hall
Weston Rhyn, 2½m north-west of
Oswestry
Tel: 0691 (Chirk) 777898
Typical small Welsh border mansion.
Open: 1 May-15 September,
Wednesday, Thursday, Saturday and
Sunday 2.30-6pm.

Wilderhope Manor
7m east of Church Stretton
Tel: 069 43 (Longville) 363
Stone Tudor house now used as youth
hostel. Interesting decoration in
principal rooms, spiral staircase, etc.
Open: April-end September,
Wednesday and Saturday 2-4.30pm;
October-March, Saturday 2-4.30pm.

MUSEUMS

See also section on Industrial and
Agricultural History

Abergavenny and District Museum
Castle House
Tel: 0873 4282
Local history, rural crafts,
reconstruction of Welsh border kitchen.
Open: March-October, Monday-
Saturday 11am-1pm and 2-5pm, Sunday
2.30-5pm; November-February,
Tuesday, Thursday, Friday and
Saturday 11am-1pm and 2-4pm.

**Automobile Palace Veteran Cycle
Collection**
Temple Street, Llandrindod Wells
Tel: 0597 2214
Collection of Veteran and Vintage
Cycles.
Open: all year, Monday-Saturday 8am-
6.30pm.

Castle Museum
Caldicot Castle
Tel: 0291 420241
Local history, costumes etc with
periodic exhibitions.
Open: March-October, daily.

Chepstow Museum
Bridge Street
Local history
Open: March-October, daily.

Churchill Gardens Museum
Fenn's Lane, Hereford
Tel: 0432 267409
Costumes, furniture, glass, porcelain,
paintings.
Open: Tuesday-Saturday 2-5pm,
Sunday, May-September 2-5pm.

Clive House
College Hill, Shrewsbury
Tel: 0743 61196
Shropshire pottery, Coalport and
Caughley porcelain. Also regimental
museum of Queen's Dragoon Guards.
Open: Monday-Saturday, daily, 10am-
5pm, except Christmas Day.

Coningsby Chapel and Museum
Widemarsh Street, Hereford
Tel: 0432 272837
Chapel of Knights of St John, also
display relating to Coningsby
Pensioners.
Open: Easter-end September, Tuesday,
Wednesday, Thursday, Saturday and
Sunday 2-5pm.

Davies Memorial Gallery
Newtown Hall Park, Newtown
Tel: 0686 26220
Local exhibitions.
Open: all year, Monday-Friday 9am-
5pm.

Dean Heritage Museum
Forest of Dean, at Upper Soudley on
B4227
Tel: 0594 22170
Forest history, traditional local crafts,
watermill.
Open: times vary, check first by ringing.

Glyn Ceiriog Memorial Institute
High Street
Collection of exhibits relating to local
cultural history and wider Welsh
interests.
Open: normally Monday-Saturday.

Gwent Rural Life Museum
New Market Street, Usk
Tel: 063 349 (Tredunnock) 315
Agriculture, domestic, crafts.
Open: April, May, June and September,
Friday, Saturday and Sunday 2-5pm;
July and August, daily 2-5pm; March
and October, Sunday 2-5pm.

Hereford City Museum and Art Gallery
Broad Street, Hereford
Tel: 0432 268121
Archaeology, natural history, costumes,
toys, militaria, folk history etc.
Open: Tuesday-Saturday 2-5pm,
Sunday, May-September 2-5pm.

**Herefordshire Light Infantry Regimental
Museum**
Harold Street, Hereford
Tel: 0432 272914
Open: by appointment, Monday-Friday.

Herefordshire Waterworks Museum
Broomy Hill, Hereford
Tel: 0432 2724104
Reconstructed Victorian waterworks,
collection of pumping engines.
Open: July and August, daily 2-5pm;
April-June and September, first Sunday
in the month.

Howell Harris Museum
Trefecca, Talgarth
1½m south of Talgarth on B4560
Exhibits relating to Howell Harris,
militant, nonconformist preacher,
pioneer agriculturalist and founder of
Trefecca community.
Open: Monday-Friday 11am-5pm;
weekends by appointment.

**King's Shropshire Light Infantry
Regimental Museum**
Sir John Moore Barracks
Copthorne Road, Shrewsbury
Tel: 0743 52234
Open: Monday-Friday 10am-12 noon
and 2-4pm.

Leominster Folk Museum
Etnam Street
Tel: 0568 2520
Open: April-October, daily; November-
March, weekends only.

Llandrindod Wells Town Museum
Memorial Gardens, Temple Street
Tel: 0597 4513
Town history, doll collection,
archaeological exhibits from Castell
Collen Roman fort.
Open: Monday-Friday 10am-12.30pm
and 2-5pm.

Llangollen Motor Museum
Sun Service Garage, Regent Street
Tel: 0978 860276
Open: Easter-end October, daily 9am-
6.30pm; winter, daily 10am-5pm.

Ludlow Museum
Butter Cross
Tel: 0584 3857
Local history, geology, zoology.
Open: Easter-end September, weekdays
10.30am-12.30pm, and 2-5pm; also
Sunday, June-August 10am-1pm, 2-5pm.
2-6pm.

Mortimer Forest Museum
Whitecliffe, Ludlow
Mainly wildlife, especially deer.
Open: all year except Bank Holidays,
Monday-Friday 9am-4pm.

Nelson Museum
Market Hall, Priory Street, Monmouth
Tel: 0600 3519
Relics of Admiral Lord Nelson and his
contemporaries. Also local history
collection.
Open: daily, all year.

The Old House
High Town, Hereford
Tel: 0432 268121 (ext 207)
Seventeenth-century house and
furniture.
Open: Tuesday-Friday 10am-1pm and
2-5.30pm, Monday and Saturday 10am-
1pm.

Powysland Museum
Church Street, Welshpool
Tel: 0938 3001
Local life and history, including Bronze
Age and Roman material. Art gallery.
Open: Monday, Tuesday and Saturday
2-4.30pm, Thursday and Friday 11am-
1pm and 2-4.30pm; also Thursday and
Friday 6-7pm, April-September.

Rowley's House Museum
Barker Street, Shrewsbury
Tel: 0743 61196
Medieval and later local history, display
of items excavated at Roman city of
Viroconium.
Open: Monday-Saturday 10am-5pm.

Shrewsbury Castle Museum
Tel: 0743 52019
Open: Easter-end September, daily
10am-5pm; October-Easter, Monday-
Saturday 10am-4pm.

Welsh Brigade Museum
Cwrt-y-Gollen barracks, 2½m south-
east of Crickhowell on A40
Tel: 0873 810386
Regimental museum of various Welsh
units (now Prince of Wales' Division).
Enquiries to guardroom.

Wolvesnewton
4m from Usk on Chepstow road (turn
off at Llangwm)
Tel: 029 15 231
Model farm, folk collection, crafts.
Open: Easter-end June, Saturday,
Sunday, Monday 11am-6pm; July-end
September, daily 11am-6pm; October-
end December, Sunday 2-5.30pm.

Included in this section are specialist
museums, working exhibitions and some
interesting former industrial sites. Many
ordinary museums, of course, have
exhibits concerned with agricultural and
industrial history.

Chirk
Telford's canal tunnel and aqueduct
over the river Ceiriog. A Victorian
railway viaduct runs parallel to the
aqueduct.

Acton Scott Farm Museum
4m south of Church Stretton off A49
Tel: 069 46 (Marshbrook) 306
Working farm demonstrating pre-
mechanised farming techniques. Rare
breeds, craft demonstrations etc.
Open: Easter-end September, Monday-
Saturday 1-6pm, Sunday and Bank
Holiday Mondays 10am-6pm.

Bacheldre Watermill
Near Church Stoke
15m east of Newtown on A489
Tel: 058 85 (Church Stoke) 489
Open: all year, weekends and most
afternoons (advisable to telephone
beforehand if travelling a distance).

Bronllys Malthouse
1½m north-west of Talgarth on B4560
Built 1885, not working but full range of
machinery and tools.
Open: all year 9am-6pm.

Bulmer Railway Centre
Whitecross Road, Hereford
Tel: 0432 276411 (Publicity Officer)
GWR steam loco *King George V* and
variety of rolling stock, including royal
coach. Occasional steam days, for
details contact Publicity Officer or
obtain the current season's leaflet from
information centre. Static displays at
other times.
Open: Easter-mid-September, Saturday
and Sunday 2-5pm.

Chwarel Wynne Slate Museum
Glyn Ceiriog
Tel: 069 172 343
Remains of old workings, underground
trips, information centre.
Open: Good Friday-end September,
10am-5pm.

Cider Museum
Ryelands Street Hereford
Tel: 0432 54207
History of traditional cider-making.
Reconstructed farm cider-house,
Cooper's shop, 1920s cider factory.
Open: daily except Tuesday and
Christmas Day 10am-5pm.

Clearwell Caves
Coleford
Former iron mines, mining equipment.
Underground tours.
Open: Easter-end September, daily
except Monday and Saturday, 10am-
5pm.

Coleham Pumping Station
Shrewsbury
Tel: 0743 62947
Built 1896-1901. Two beam engines on
view.
Open: Whitsun-September, daily except
Monday 10am-4pm.

Ellesmere Canal Wharf
Canal wharf in town (former depot of
Shropshire Union). Junction of
Montgomery Canal and Shropshire
Union at Welsh Frankton, 4m west on
A495, now being restored.

Glyn Valley Tramway
Glyn Ceiriog
Tel: 069 172 210
Small exhibition of memorabilia at Glyn
Valley Hotel.

Hendre Granite Quarry
$2\frac{1}{2}$m west of Glyn Ceiriog. Access by
path between Pandy and Tregeiriog.

Grindley Brook Locks
2m north of Whitchurch on A41
Busy flight of locks in summer months.

Grinshill Quarries
$4\frac{1}{2}$m south of Wem
Famous source of high quality building
stone.

Llangollen Canal Museum
The Wharf, Llangollen
Tel: 0978 860702
Canal history displays, souvenirs,
bookstall. Narrowboat trips (horse-
drawn).
Open: Easter-end September, daily;
boat trips July and August, each
afternoon; April-June and September,
most weekend afternoons.

Llangollen Station
Tel: 0978 860951
Station and stretch of line restored by
preservation society. Occasional steam
trips. Opening times vary.

Llangynog, Tanat Valley
Former mining and quarrying village
surrounded by old workings, machinery
etc.

Llanymynech Hill
6m south on A483
Nineteenth-century limestone quarrying
area, old machinery and workings,
Roman mines. Free access.

Newtown Textile Museum
Commercial Street
Tel: 0686 26243
Machinery and exhibits of former
woollen industry, housed in old weaving
shops.
Open: April-October, Tuesday-
Saturday, 2-4.30pm.

Norchard Steam Centre
1m north of Lydney on B4234
Tel: 0594 43423
Collection of locos, coaches and
wagons, steam trips.
Open: static display, every day; rides,
June-September, Sunday and Bank
Holidays.

Oswestry Station Yard
Platforms, signal-boxes, loco and
carriage works. Cambrian Railway
Society restores engines and rolling
stock in yard nearby.
Open: most weekends.

Pontcysyllte Aqueduct
5m east of Llangollen
Telford's aqueduct is accessible from the
canal basin at Trevor and is 120ft high
and 1,000ft long.

Snailbeach and Shelve
Under Stiperstones range, west of Long
Mynd.
Many relics of lead mining industry.
Free access.

Watermill (DOE)
Mortimer's Cross, Leominster
Open: Thursday afternoons.

Welshpool and Llanfair Light Railway
Raven Square terminus, Welshpool
Tel: (HQ) 0938 (Llanfair Caereinion)
810441
Restored 2ft 6in gauge line with
interesting variety of locos and rolling
stock. Headquarters, with display, at
Llanfair Caereinion, western end of line.

RELIGIOUS FOUNDATIONS

Abbey Cwmhir
6m north of Llandrindod Wells on A483
Site, with some remains, of one of the
largest medieval abbeys.

Abbey Dore
11m south-west of Hereford on A465
Site of Cistercian abbey. Large restored
church survives.

Hereford Cathedral
Many features of interest, but
particularly notable are the large
chained library and the *Mappa Mundi* - a
medieval map of the world.

Llanthony Abbey
3m north of Llanthony Priory at Capel-
y-Ffin
Ruins of short-lived monastic
community church, late nineteenth
century. Contains tomb of founder, the
Revd Josephy Leycester Lyne (Father
Ignatius). Residential quarters survive,
privately owned.

Llanthony Priory (DOE)
Vale of Ewyas
B4423 off A465 north-east of
Abergavenny
Ruins of eleventh/twelfth-century
Priory. Mainly church and gatehouse.
Former Prior's lodging is now hotel.
Former infirmary is St David's parish
church.

Shrewsbury Abbey Church
Apart from the church, little survives
following routing of Holyhead road
through ruins. Refectory pulpit can still
be seen on other side of road.

Tintern Abbey (DOE)
Open: mid-March to mid-October,
weekdays 9.30am-6.30pm; Sunday
2-4pm, April-September 9.30am-
6.30pm; rest of year, weekdays 9.30am-
4pm, Sunday 2-4pm.

Valle Crucis
Llangollen
Extensive ruins of Cistercian abbey.
Open: May-end September, daily.

Wigmore Abbey
Leintwardine
A4113 west of Ludlow
Tel: Mrs Scott, 056 886 454.
Twelfth-century Augustinian
foundation. Remains include gatehouses
and former Abbots' lodging.
Open: by appointment only.

Parish Churches and Chapels

All parish churches have something to
attract the visitor, but the following are
of exceptional interest.

Abergavenny Priory Church
Chepstow - St Mary's
Clyro
Cwmyoy (Vale of Ewyas)
Grosmont
Hereford - All Saints
Hewelsfield (2m south of St Briavels on
B4228)
Kilpeck
Leominster Priory Church
Llananno (south of Newtown)
Llangwm - St Jerome's (4m from Usk on
Chepstow road)
Llanyblodwell (Tanat Valley)
Ludlow
Maesyronnen Chapel (near Glasbury)
Mathern (1m south-west of Chepstow)
Newland (4m south-east of Monmouth)
Old Radnor
Pales Quaker Meeting House (near
Llandegley)
Pennant Melangell (near Llangynog)
Ross - St Mary's
Shrewsbury - St Mary's, St Chad's,
Battlefield.
St Margaret's (near Ewyas Harold)
Staunton (3m east of Monmouth on
A4136)
Tidenham (2m north-east of Chepstow
on A48)
Trellech (5m south of Monmouth on
B4293)

Craft Workshops

At all the following establishments
visitors are welcome to look at work in
production.

Alaven Designs
Cymric Mill, Canal Road, Newtown
Tel: 0686 26342
Leather goods and other craft products.
Open: all year, Monday-Friday, 9am-
5.30pm, Saturday by appointment.

Grahame Amey Ltd
The Granary, Standard Street,
Crickhowell
Tel: 0873 810540
Hand-made furniture.
Open: Monday-Friday, 8am-5.30pm and
most Saturday mornings, or by
appointment.

Black Mountain Pottery
Llanelieu Court
2½m east of Talgarth
Tel: 0874 711518
Domestic stoneware, drawings and
paintings.
Open: any reasonable time, telephone in
advance.

Cambrian factory
Llanwrtyd Wells, west of Builth on A483
Tel: 059 13 211
Large mill, staffed by disabled people.
Welsh tweeds and woollens.
Open: Monday-Friday, 8.15am-5.30pm;
shop, Saturday and Bank Holiday in
summer months, 9am-4.30pm.

Crefftau Ceiriog
Glyn Ceiriog
Tel: 069 172 218
Hand-made furniture.
Open: summer, Monday-Friday, 9am-
5pm; other times by appointment.

George Dear Pottery
Upper Lion
Colourful stoneware.
Open: July-end September, Monday-
Friday 9am-6pm (shop at weekends as
well); October-June, Monday-Friday
9am-5.30pm, Bank Holidays 10am-6pm.

**Fiddlers Folly Puppet Workshop and
Theatre**
2m south of Church Stretton on B4370
Tel: 06946 (Marshbrook) 300
Production of puppets and
performances.
Open: June-end October, weekends and
Bank Holidays, 10am-5pm.
Book for performances.

G.J. and H.M. Frode
Llanfared, Builth Wells
1½m from Builth on A481
Hand-turned woodwork.

The Gallery
Hillersland, Coleford
Paintings and pottery.
Open: during normal business hours.

Hildre Pottery
Hengoed, Oswestry
3m north-west of Oswestry off Weston
Rhyn road.

Llangollen Pottery
Regent Street, Llangollen
Tel: 0978 860249
Domestic stoneware.
Open: March-October, daily 9am-6pm.

Llangollen Weavers
Dee Lane, Llangollen
Tel: 0978 860630
Old cornmill with waterwheel.
Demonstrations of weaving on old
loom.
Open: shop, Easter-end October, daily,
Monday-Saturday in winter months;
demonstrations, Monday-Friday.

Log Cabin Crafts Centre
Llandogo, near Tintern
Tel: 059 453 (St Briavels) 355
Pottery, baskets, jewellery, leather,
candles.
Open: daily, except Tuesday, 10am-
dusk.

Mid-Wales House
Llanavon Road, Newbridge-on-Wye
Tel: 059 789 364
Spinning, weaving, hand-knitting.

Stuart Perkins Pottery
The Scowles, Bream
Tel: 0594 (Dean) 33570
Visits by arrangement.

Penybont Pottery
North-east of Llandrindod Wells on
A44.

Royal forest of Dean Pottery
Bream, near Lydney
Tel: 0594 (Dean) 562414
Open: daily, 9.30am-1pm, 2-5.30pm.

Terracopia Pottery
Pontfadog, Glyn Ceiriog
East of Glyn Ceiriog
Terracotta products.

The Welsh Gallery
18 Cross Street, Abergavenny
Tel: 0873 4023
Work by various Welsh artists and
craftsmen.

Wye Pottery
Clyro, Hay-on-Wye
Tel: 0497 510
Unusual earthenware pottery.
Open: Monday-Saturday and Bank
Holidays, 9am-1pm, 3-6pm, Sunday by
appointment.

INFORMATION CENTRES

All the Centres on the following list
stock the standard tourist literature, and
those marked with an asterisk operate
the bed-booking service for visitors who
have failed to make advance
arrangements (a small charge is made
for this).

*Abergavenny, 2 Lower Monk Street
Tel: 0873 3254
(Also Brecon Beacons National Park
Centre)

*Builth Wells, Main car park
Tel: 098 22 3307

*Chepstow, The Gatehouse, High Street
Tel: 02912 3772

Church Stretton, Church Street
Tel: 0694 722535
(Shropshire Hills Information Centre)

Cinderford, Library, Belle Vue Road
Tel: 0594 2258

*Hereford, Shire Hall
Tel: 0432 268430

Knighton, West Street
Tel: 0547 528573
(Also Offa's Dyke Centre)

Leominster, Corn Square
Tel: 0568 2291

*Llandrindod Wells, Town Hall
Tel: 0597 2260

Llangollen, Town Hall
Tel: 0978 860828

Ludlow, Castle Street
Tel: 0584 3857

*Monmouth, National Trust Shop,
Church Street
Tel: 0600 3899

*Newtown, Central car park
Tel: 0686 25580

*Oswestry, Library
Tel: 0691 62753

*Ross, 20 Broad Street
Tel: 0989 62768

*Shrewsbury, The Square
Tel: 0743 52019

Talgarth, Bruton House
Tel: 087 481 586

*Tintern, The Abbey
Tel: 02918 431

*Welshpool, Main car park
Tel: 0938 2043

*Whitchurch, Civic Centre
Tel: 0948 3403

Youth Hostels

The Regional Office of the YHA is at
Woodville Road, Cardiff, Tel: 0222
31370.

Capel-y-Ffin Y.H.
Abergavenny, Gwent, NP7 7NP
Tel: 087 382 (Crucorney) 650

Chepstow Y.H.
Mountain Road, Chepstow,
Gwent, NP6 6AA
Tel: 029 12 2685

Knighton Y.H.
Old Primary School, West Street,
Knighton, Powys, LD7 1EN
Tel: 0547 528807

Llanbedr Y.H.
Plas Newydd, Llanbedr,
Gwynedd, LL45 2LE
Tel: 034 123 287

Llangollen Y.H.
Tyndwr Hall, Tyndwr Road,
Llangollen, Clwyd, LL20 8AR
Tel: 0978 860330

Ludlow Y.H.
Ludford Lodge, Ludford,
Ludlow, Salop, SY8 1PJ
Tel: 0584 2472

Mitcheldean Y.H.
Lion House, High Street,
Micheldean, Glos. GL17 0AT
Tel: 0594 (Dean) 542366

Monmouth Y.H.
Priory Street School, Priory Street,
Monmouth, Gwent, NP5 3NX
Tel: 0600 5116

Shrewsbury Y.H.
The Woodlands, Abbey Foregate,
Shrewsbury, SY2 6LZ
Tel: 0743 56397

St Briavels Castle Y.H.
The Castle, St Briavels,
Lydney, Glos. GL15 6RG
Tel: 0594 530829

Welsh Bicknor Y.H.
Welsh Bicknor Rectory,
Welsh Bicknor, Ross-on-Wye,
Herefordshire, HR9 6JJ
Tel: 0594 (Dean) 60300

Wales Tourist Board
Brunel House, Fitzalan Road,
Cardiff, CF2 1UY
Tel: 0222 499909

British Tourist Authority
64 St James Street,
London, SW1A 1NF
Tel: 01 409 0969
For Wales only

English Tourist Board
4 Grosvenor Gardens,
London, SW1W 0DU
Tel: 01 730 3400

Heart of England Tourist Board
PO Box 15,
Worcester, WR1 2JT
Tel: 0905 29511

National Trust
42 Queen Anne's Gate,
London, SW1H 9AS
Tel: 01 222 9251

Ramblers Association
1-5 Wandsworth Road,
London, SW8 2LJ
Tel: 01 582 6878

Forestry Commission
Churchill House, Churchill Way,
Cardiff
Tel: 0222 40661

Camping Club
of Great Britain and Ireland
11 Grosvenor Place,
London, SW1W 0EY
Tel: 01 828 1012

Cyclists Touring Club
69 Meadrow,
Godalming,
Surrey
Tel: 048 68 7217

Welsh Water Authority
Headquarters, Cambrian Way,
Brecon, LD3 7HP
Tel: 0874 3181

Usk Division
Station Buildings,
Queensway, Newport,
Gwent
Tel: 0633 840404

Wye Division
St Nicholas House, St Nicholas Street,
Hereford
Tel: 0432 57411

Severn Trent Water Authority
Upper Severn Division,
Shelton, Shrewsbury
Tel: 0743 63141

The above offices give information
about public fishing rights, licences
needed etc in the Border area. In
addition there is 24hr recorded
information about fishing conditions —
see WATER in the local telephone book.

Index